W9-CBN-282

How To
Stop Feeling Blue

How To
Stop Feeling
Blue

by

Frank Cheavens, Ph.D.

Professor of Psychology
University of Texas
at Arlington

A World of Books That Fill a Need

Frederick Fell, Inc.   *New York*

TO

My wife, Lula Lee,
out of gratitude for her love and loyalty

Contents

How To
Stop Feeling Blue

Introduction:
The Outlook Is Hopeful

FROM TIME TO TIME you find yourself trapped by the blues and it isn't a good feeling. As you realize this, you may get some small comfort from knowing that these periods of gloom are very general, perhaps about as general as the common cold. And like the common cold they are a terrible bother. The good word here is that you really can banish those blues! You can do it once and for all and completely.

I have a friend who was periodically cursed by depression. Now he has evolved his own system of preventing the blues. Or if he falls victim to an attack, he deals with it quickly and successfully, so that it is of the briefest duration. In like manner, you can evolve your own strategy for beating the blues.

Moods May Run in Cycles

One early investigator kept records of the fluctuations in mood of twelve workingmen.[1] He discovered that among these men there were definite cycles. The time spread from the bottom of depression to the peak of optimism ranged from three to nine weeks. Many people have observed in themselves a fairly regular and almost predictable occurrence of moods of melancholy. Some have even noticed that they are more subject to depression during certain seasons of the year.

Two other investigators, using college men as subjects, arrived at conclusions that were in close agreement.[2,3] Melancholy feelings were worst during the winter months and feelings of happiness highest during spring and summer. Monday was the bluest day of the week. The first and last half hours of the day were the lowest periods of any given day.

You might find it profitable to keep a record of your low periods and your high periods and everything connected with each extreme swing of mood. If you can establish the pattern of recurrence of your blues it might help in their cure. Finding this pattern, you might get at causes. Also, if you knew approximately when your spell of gloom was going to take over, you could begin to take preventive measures.

Other studies which have been made have not established that moods occur in cycles. We have to assume that with some people there may be no regularity of depressed periods, but with others there is. If you can't establish a time schedule, this will not keep you from learning to counteract low morale when it hits you.

The Handicaps of Low Morale

Periods of low morale are a serious handicap in many ways, and it is very doubtful whether they are ever beneficial. Some people report a "sweet melancholy," which seems to be a sort of mixture of sadness and mild pleasure. Most of us would rather take our pleasure unadulterated!

In business and industry low morale seems to be a combination of resentment and disappointment due to various frustrations, and low morale is clearly linked to low productivity in groups of workers. Likewise your poor morale will usually bring about inefficiency in your work and smaller productivity in your unique line of achievement. Eventually this may mean that your earnings will also be down. All of this can be avoided.

Apparently your body cannot function at its best during depression. You will immediately recognize that there is an interaction here. If your body is not functioning well, you may be more subject to depression, but despondency also contributes to the malfunction of your body. Either could come first, and taking care of both the physiological and psychological factors is necessary for best results.

Human relations that are satisfying seem to be necessary for most people if life is to be happy and successful. When you have the blues you will usually not be at your best socially. Your relations with your family will not be as rewarding as when your spirits are high, and relations between husband and wife are also often adversely affected. The same will be true with your other friends or associates, including those having to do with your business or profession.

One of your greatest drawbacks due to these "bad" days or periods is that during them you may cheat yourself out of tackling some enterprise that would be highly successful and gratifying. When you are in the dumps confidence is at a low ebb and you will be afraid to try anything new.

Again, as with your physical well-being mentioned before, interacting forces are set up. You refuse to take the new promising job because your confidence is weak, and this refusal in turn makes you feel worse, which in turn causes your relations with other people to be below par, which again increases your feeling of depression. Your productivity is also lowered and this knowledge adds to your negative feelings. All of this adds up to the hard fact that sagging morale is just plain no good!

But the outlook is hopeful. Having picked up this book is one good sign that you are motivated to improve your situation. This positive motivation is one of the big steps in your banishing these periods of gloom from your life, and you may be sure that it can be done!

There are many strategies for dealing with despondency.

Some of these have been tried out on a broad scale with a high percentage of success. Others have not been tried as widely but have helpful elements in them, particularly for certain types of people.

The Strategies that Will Be Presented Will
Help You to Help Yourself

The only real help we usually can give anyone is to help the person to help himself. This is true even in medical science where the physician gives the human body needed help so that the body can heal itself.

In this book, a number of ways of coping with depression will be described. Out of these you may try those which seem the most workable and from them select those which succeed. You can design your own strategy and begin to work at it. As you experiment you may discard certain methods that do not seem productive and adopt others that seem more promising.

Later you may wish to go back over this book to see if you missed anything that gives promise of working. Your experiences should be a continuing education with increasing success in managing your emotions.

Also you may find certain techniques very useful for a while and then discover that you have developed to the point where you have outgrown your need for that particular method.

Not only will the skills in self-management you learn apply to depression but also to other emotions that you find hard to handle, such as needless fear, anger, and anxiety. In many ways these so-called negative emotions are all very closely related.

Many of the ways of counteracting or preventing depression come from the work of clinicians with people who are classified as neurotics. The neurotic person is usually one whose life is more seriously disorganized and disrupted by emotional disturbance than the average person who has emotional problems. In fact, it is sometimes hard for us to say who is neurotic and who is not. We are coming closer all the time to less emphasis on such classifications. Each individual is unique. He may be a person with serious problems who needs a boost no matter how he may be classified.

Anyway, some of the methods drawn from the clinic are usually in some part very applicable to the average person with emotional problems. In many cases we can infer that if this method works with neurotic people, it also ought to work with a person not so seriously disturbed.

Cases of Severe Depression Require
Expert Professional Help

Depression sometimes gets so out of hand, becoming so serious that help from highly trained professionals is required. This book is not written with any idea of keeping a person who has such a serious illness from consulting with a psychiatrist. Rather, a strong recommendation is here made that such a disturbed person *should* consult a psychiatrist as soon as it can possibly be arranged.

Even so, your psychiatrist may want you to read this book as an adjunct to therapy. It is hoped that these pages will prove helpful to psychiatrists and psychologists in the process of treating disturbed people. It should stimulate helpful questions from time to time, and it should also aid the patient in understanding what the psychotherapist is trying to do. Later in the book a brief chapter will be devoted to a discussion of neurotic depressions and those even more severe disturbances which we describe as psychotic.

In the main, as much as we hope this book can also help the severely depressed, it is intended for those of you who are bothered with periodic blues or allied emotions that keep you from being your best self and from doing your best work.

It sometimes takes a very small margin to make a vast difference in the way things turn out. The size of a piston can be off a very little bit and you burn up your motor. A small margin makes the difference between a smooth-running engine and one with damaging friction. If the blades on a pair of scissors are a shade too tight or a shade too loose, they just won't cut well at all. A small fraction of an inch many times decides whether a door will open or close. Likewise, a very small margin of change in your emotions may make the difference in how you get along with your fellow beings and may also give you that margin of freedom and power you need to achieve your goals.

---

[1] Hersey, R. B. "Rate of Production and Emotional State." *Personnel Journal*, 1932, 10, 355-364.

[2] Cason, H. "General Curves and Conditions of Feeling." *Journal of Applied Psychology*, 1931, 15, 126-148.

[3] Springer, N. N. and Roslow, S. "A Study in the Estimation of Feelings." *Journal of Applied Psychology*, 1935, 19, 379-384.

CHAPTER 1.

Getting at Causes May Help

IN CHAPTER 2 we will present a practical strategy that ought to help you as long as you live. But there is a line of thinking that needs to be introduced in order for you to get the full benefit from Chapter 2. This has to do with the causes of depression.

There was a time when some people, not too well-informed, felt that if you knew the cause or causes of your emotional trouble, the trouble would magically vanish. This was in part due to the fact that in some exceptional cases this actually happened. The person found the hidden cause for his difficulty and the difficulty almost seemed to melt like butter in the hot sunshine.

In many psychiatric films this sort of thing made for a dramatic story. Here was a character who had an unconquerable fear. The psychiatrist, then, played the role of a

19

scholarly detective, tracking down the mysterious cause. The impressive climax was reached when finally the mastermind found the mysterious source of the trouble after which the irrational fear disappeared.

Well, it makes an interesting story!

This is not usually the way these things happen, but we can still say that knowing causes will help. Usually you have to go beyond such knowledge, however, to solve the problem. But as one of the steps toward the solution of your emotional problem, this insight into the "why" of the problem is important.

Most of the causes of your spells of blueness will fall under three classifications. One is that there are things that happen to us from our environment that give us the blues. The second is there are those events from within you, from your mind, from the way your personality was formed, that make you feel bad. And third you may become downcast because of some combination of the external and internal forces.

External Causes

Financial reverses may give you the blues. You have bought stock in a reliable company. This company has bad reverses and the price goes down. You are disappointed.

I have a friend whose daughter received serious burns in a car accident. Her recovery was in doubt for some time.

When she did recover she required extensive plastic surgery and it will take her father years to pay the bills which ran into many thousands of dollars. This whole series of events is enough to cause a person to feel low.

And one thing none of us can escape is the sorrow that comes from the loss of someone loved dearly. If this person was a lifetime companion, a huge gap is left in your life that is hard to fill.

If one is very sensitive he may feel hurt because of some social slight. He wasn't invited to the big banquet, but most of his friends were. Or he finds out that someone whose friendship he valued highly is gradually dropping him. Pride is hurt. There seems to be little he can do about it, so he becomes depressed.

I know a young woman who was confidently expecting an invitation to join a certain social club. The invitation never came, and it took her a long time to get over this blow to her morale.

Hardly anyone escapes certain occupational disappointments. Others are advanced more rapidly than you are. Others get better raises. Or you expected to enjoy your chosen work and now it has become a dull routine. Or you have advanced as far as you will ever go and this knowledge saddens you. Or again your chosen work doesn't pay as good a living as you might wish.

Physical troubles also play their part in causing a person to feel dejected. Most of us can react with some optimism to a passing illness. Your head cold makes you feel miserable but you know you'll be better in a day or two. You ate something that poisoned you, but you knew you would soon be over it.

But how about a person who learns that he is diabetic and will continue to be for the rest of his life. I know of several cases of people who have been disabled from automobile accidents which were entirely the other fellow's fault. They have been left handicapped for life because of the carelessness or neglect of another person.

There are also those happenings which are caused by our own blunders, our own failures and mistakes. I know a man who ran over and killed a child. He has never quite recovered from his tragic mistake.

All of these are things that happen to us. We may have something to do with them ourselves. In any case, they are losses, disappointments, or frustrations and we clearly know what they are. And we can understand the reason the blue-devils dance around us.

Internal Causes

The second kind of cause is not as easy to see, but it is just as real, and is usually harder to deal with because it is more complicated. Here the cause for the blues may go a long way back and has become almost a built-in part of your personality.

Let's take an example. I know a young woman, Mrs. Ethel Z. (not her real name), who was having frequent spells of despondency. She was an only child. Her father had deserted her mother when Ethel was quite young, and her mother was not always as warm and loving to Ethel as she should have been.

The daughter became unsure of her mother's love and this frightened her. It frightened her so much that she was afraid to do anything without her mother's approval. Ethel was so insecure that she failed to develop her own necessary independence.

Now along with these troubles the daughter couldn't help having a certain amount of rebellion against her mother. At times she disliked what her mother did but was afraid to admit this dislike to herself. Her hostility toward her mother made Ethel feel too guilty even to admit it to herself.

Whenever she felt any anger toward her mother, Ethel felt she was a sinful person and unworthy. Later, when she married, her mother still tried to run her life. Ethel resented this, but her resentment made her feel that she was almost criminal to have such thoughts about her mother.

So why does she have the blues so often? Because she is trying to become independent of her mother and because she feels guilt whenever she gets angry because of her mother's bossiness.

With this type of depression, you have at least three emotions. One is fear. Guilt is a type of fear. The guilt is a result of a feeling of hostility, which is anger. The depression occurs because the daughter feels she is a wicked person to feel angry and hostile toward her own mother. And all of it started before the daughter can even remember. And many of these feelings are now habits. What can she do about it? This will be discussed later.

Ethel's blues are due to things that happened to her, but mainly having to do with people very close to her over a long period of time and beginning in early childhood. Also her emotion isn't sadness alone. It is sadness coupled with fear and hostility.

Let's take another example, the case of Mr. X. He has worked for a certain firm a long time. The boss, who has his troubles, too, has grown harder and harder to deal with. Many times the boss blames Mr. X for errors which are not his fault. Mr. X has become increasingly depressed over his work.

But here is a complicating factor. When Mr. X was a boy, his father was an arbitrary, dictatorial figure, something like the boss. But Mr. X as a boy was afraid of his father. He never answered him back or took up for himself. He harbored deep feelings of resentment against his father, but he also felt guilty about these feelings. He felt that his resentment of his father was a horrible sin, so he kept those feelings of resentment down and never expressed them.

Now in the case of his boss, not only does Mr. X feel blue about working conditions and unfair treatment, but all of those early feelings of guilt about disliking his father have become active again. One reason Mr. X feels depressed is because he feels he is a bad person to feel angry at his boss.

Combination of External and Internal Causes

In this last case we have an example of the third and last type of cause of the blues where some depressing circumstance in the present combines with personality formation of the past to create depression.

Another example of this combination is the case of a middle-aged woman whom we shall call Alma. Alma had four children, each about eighteen months apart, and they came early in her marriage. When Alma was forty her husband was killed.

Alma's childhood had been unhappy. She had felt neglected and unloved. When she had married she devoted herself completely to her husband, her children, and her duties as a homemaker. But by the time she was fifty, all of her children had left home, and so Alma found herself going through the menopause, and in a few years time she was completely deserted by those she had devoted her life and energies to. Her depression was caused partly by her early personality formation, partly by the death of her husband, partly by the fact that her children had matured and left home. In addition to this was the natural occurrence of physical changes due to the menopause.

Outside of her family, Alma had developed hardly any interests. Now she found herself looking at a bleak and lonely future, feeling that all the best of her life was behind her. The death of her husband and the departure of her children reactivated her childhood feelings of being neg-lected and deserted.

By setting down these three major types of causes of low feelings, we don't mean to leave the impression that you can neatly catalogue each type of the blues. But perhaps this short description of causes will help you understand your periods of low morale better. And it is both comforting and encouraging to be able to find causes.

What we are interested in chiefly is what to do about the mopes when we are caught by them. So we shall plunge immediately into one very practical method that can be self-taught.

CHAPTER 2.

You Can Learn to Turn Loose: The Jacobson Method

DEPRESSION IS ALMOST WITHOUT EXCEPTION preceded by, as well as accompanied by, anxiety. In anxiety there is a definite tensing of many muscles of the body. These muscular tensions become habitual.

Fortunately, we have sensitive electrical instruments that can show the existence of these tensions. If you are in a state of mental and emotional anxiety you are also in a state of considerable muscular tension. And this tension can be measured.

It is hard to separate mental from emotional or from muscular tension. For practical purposes all you need to know is that if you learn to relax your muscular tensions, this helps remedy the emotional and mental states. For much of this practical knowledge we are indebted to a medical doctor who is also a highly trained physiologist, Dr. Edmund Jacobson.

Dr. Jacobson is a man who has translated his theoretical knowledge into a useful, easily learned method of learning to relax. This method is systematic, and must be well learned. It is a skill, and like any other skill it requires considerable practice before you become good at it. But with practice you can become an expert. You can learn the method from a book. Of course, it might be more quickly learned if you had an instructor who could demonstrate it to you, and it might be more fun if you were a member of a class and all of your group learned it simultaneously.

If the reader is a woman and is fortunate enough to be pregnant usually she can find, in nearby urban centers, classes of training for natural childbirth. One of the basic skills taught in these classes is the Jacobson method of Progressive Relaxation. Pain and muscular tension also seem to be related. The more tense you are, the worse pain becomes and the harder to bear. Training the mother-to-be in systematic relaxation has been very successful in reducing pain during childbirth.[1]

But if you have no instructor available and no class you can join, this method is explicit enough so that you can learn it entirely on your own.

Without going into great detail here, we can give you the general idea of how you learn this system.[2] To get the instructions in complete form, borrow one of the Jacobson books from your public library or buy one. Most libraries consider these books of great enough usefulness to include them on their shelves.

You stretch out on a bed in a comfortable position on your back with legs uncrossed. You start with one arm and tense the muscles in that arm. Then you turn them loose. Let the arm go completely limp. And although this is not necessary, for various reasons my own opinion is that before you relax or as you relax you should think of a word or words that can later become useful as signals. "Relax" is fine or "turn loose" or "loosen up." Tensing the arm muscles takes effort, but relaxing takes none at all. Your arm lies there with no effort.

This procedure of contracting the arm muscles and relaxing them should be practiced several times. As the person does this, other body muscles should not be tensed. Sometimes as you concentrate on your arm, your face or other muscles may be tensing.

Now you should practice letting this arm go limp without previously contracting the muscles. Let it be fun. Relaxing is not work; it is a refusal to work. All of it is undoing. None of it is doing. Look forward to feeling rested and happy after your period of practice.

You proceed from one arm to the other. Breathing should be normally regular and relaxed as you proceed. How fast you proceed with this learning depends upon you. You should try to find several periods during each day when you can practice. You might proceed from your hands and arms to your feet and legs; then to abdominal and chest muscles. Face and scalp muscles are also important. Neck and shoulder muscles are, with many people, regions of great tension. You can learn to relax all over.

Eventually you proceed to every set of muscles in your body. Personally, I like to think of the word "relax" as I turn loose each part of my body. And after long practice I can give myself the signal word *relax* whenever I find myself tense, and at the signal all the muscles of my body begin to loosen up.

In many of the classes of instruction they begin with one hand and arm and you practice only that several times a day. At the next lesson you take the other hand and arm and, following this lesson, practice with both hands and arms several times a day.

In a gradual way, you extend your practice to the muscles of the entire body. After much practice you can stretch out and think the word "relax" with one arm and then the other. Next, perhaps you go to your feet and legs and proceed to your stomach, shoulder and neck muscles, and then the muscles of your face and scalp. The order in which you relax the muscles is not important.

I have a student who suffered from insomnia. Now, after only short periods of practicing Progressive Relaxation, when he goes to bed he gives himself the signal "relax" and needs nothing further. His muscles all turn loose and almost immediately he falls off to sleep.

For those who demand experimental demonstration of results, Jacobson has directed a number of studies which may be found reported in the scholarly journals. Also in his book, *Progressive Relaxation*, some of these are briefly described.

For example, he studied five subjects who "had clear histories of severe nervous symptoms but who had been trained to relax."[3] Most of their varied symptoms disappeared after relaxation training. One of these subjects had shown the symptoms of depression.

Jacobson also conducted experiments in which he measured the electrical potentials from subjects who were being trained, comparing each subject's training record with his record prior to training. Not satisfied with this, the investigator used a group of "controls," subjects who did not have the training but who were trying to relax. The records are photographic tracings from the galvanometer indicating the amount of muscular tension. The control subjects' records are unmistakable in demonstrating the control group's inability to relax well without training. The training group's record showed a distinct reduction in muscular tensions due to training.

Many similar studies were made, some of them with large numbers of subjects. In everyday language, the results of these experiments indicated at least three rather clear results: (1) Without training, most people don't relax very well even when they are trying; (2) with training most people achieve success in relaxation that can be scientifically demonstrated; and (3) people with "nervous" symptoms who are trained can successfully learn to relax and their symptoms seem to be reduced.

Jacobson has taken thousands of these records related to relaxation and tension, enough to convince the most hardheaded skeptics.

Three Psychiatrists Who Use the
Jacobson Method

Three psychiatrists, all of them teachers in a medical school, Drs. Haugen, Dixon, and Dickel, have tried to work out a system that the average general practitioner can use with people who are "nervous."

Simply stated they have concluded, with considerable supporting evidence, that "anxiety reactions" are learned, and in many anxious people, this learning perhaps started in childhood. This anxiety is characterized by overly tense muscles. Just as this tension was learned, relaxation can also be learned.[4]

A relationship between this anxiety and depression is also suggested. They take the typical example of a housewife who is overtaxed with too great a variety of demanding responsibilities. She becomes fatigued and irritable, quarrels with her husband because of her tension, and afterward has a real case of the blues. As stated in the preceding chapter, it seems that most depression is preceded by or accompanied by some sort of anxiety, and this means excessive tensions.[5]

So the first steps these doctors take is to teach this person the Jacobson method of relaxation. When he has learned this system, the next step is to get him to practice it during all sorts of normal daytime activities. He may practice it while watching television, while working at the office, or during almost any of his usual pursuits.[6]

One of their typical cases was a middle-aged man who

had strange "ballooning" sensations in his head. He had many other bodily complaints such as painful tensions in his shoulder and neck muscles, blurring of vision, and digestive upsets. He had also been subject to depression and insomnia. His symptoms had been so disturbing that he had been unable to work for several weeks.

The major emphasis in treatment was to teach him Progressive Relaxation. After a number of practice sessions by himself he was asked to demonstrate his ability to his teacher and it was affirmed that he was following the right procedure. Later he reported falling asleep after finishing his exercises.

At his fourth report he had become very enthusiastic at having lost most of his symptoms. He had previously been forewarned of possible setbacks. One of these came some weeks later at the death of his mother. Following this many of his former symptoms reappeared. But his most bothersome symptom was depression. He was instructed to return as soon as possible to his former practice of Progressive Relaxation. This he did with success and again began to lose his symptoms. He began laying plans for the future and after several weeks had regained his lost ground and was again relatively free from symptoms.

In a few more weeks he had gone back to work and was sleeping and eating well. In about another month when he reported back he said that most of his tensions and other symptoms were no longer bothering him and that he was experiencing considerable success in his work. Six months of reporting back indicated that he had his personal situation well in hand.

This is an abbreviated acount of what happened, but it is enough to show the effects of learning systematic relaxation.

This man could be classified as a neurotic, a case of anxiety reaction. He was also depressed. This diagnosis is not too important for our purpose here. It means that his disturbance had reached a point where it was disrupting his normal activities, including his work. He sought expert medical help, as he should have, was treated, and was relieved of his disorganizing symptoms by a simple method.

If this relaxation method will work with as severe a case as his, the average person with milder anxiety and depression surely could expect as good results, and perhaps achieve them more quickly. Of course, it takes practice to learn the skill and constant application after it has been learned.

The only way you can determine whether this plan will be of benefit to you is to give it a real trial over a period of several months. Our prediction is that you will find it to be of great benefit to you in many ways.

There will be more references to the Jacobson method in later chapters. This is only one of a number of strategies from which you can evolve your own individual system of maintaining high morale.

Haugen, Dixon, and Dickel feel that they have a system which can be applied by the busy general practitioner. A nurse or a physiotherapist or almost any other intelligent lay person can learn to teach Progressive Relaxation, thus relieving the physician. It is emphasized, however, that the physician who applies this method must first learn the Jacobson method in order to know whether it is being correctly taught and learned. This will also help the doctor who himself needs to learn how to relax.

These three investigators claim only to have demonstrated that this is a promising method. They claim to have "proved" nothing. However, Dr. Jacobson himself with his earlier studies has added to the reliable evidence that this is a beneficial method.

You can definitely learn to turn loose. This will be beneficial to your emotions. The anxiety which usually lies behind the depression will lessen.

With lessened muscular tensions you will be in a better frame of mind to solve your problems intelligently. Your thinking will be more flexible, and flexibility in thinking is a prerequisite to clear problem-solving.

Relaxation is one very practical device in beating the blues and in solving all your emotional problems. You can learn this skill and practice it and give yourself a definite boost in a positive direction.

---

[1] Read, Grantley Dick. *Childbirth Without Fear.*

[2] Jacobson, Edmund. *Progressive Relaxation.* Chicago: The University of Chicago Press, 1956, pp. 40-80.

[3] _____. *You Must Relax.* New York: McGraw-Hill, 1948.

[4] *Ibid.,* pp. 314-326.

[5] Haugen, G. B., Dixon, H. H., and Dickel, H. A. *A Therapy for Anxiety Tension Reactions.* New York: The Macmillian Company, 1960.

[6] *Ibid.,* pp. 15-16.

CHAPTER 3.

A Practical Method:
Alfred Adler's Approach

ONE OF THE GREATEST and most practical pioneers in helping people deal successfully with their emotional difficulties was one of Sigmund Freud's younger associates, Dr. Alfred Adler. He called his system Individual Psychology.

Adler felt, quite differently from Freud, that the findings of psychology could be shared with the great masses of humanity. When Adler returned from his service as a military doctor at the Russian front during World War I, he was a changed man. Some of his former ideas had now become fully developed and carried much greater weight with him.

On returning from war duty to civilian life in Vienna, Adler was reunited with his friends in the cafe society of Vienna. When they first saw Adler, they immediately wanted

to know what new thing he had discovered in his absence
that he could share with them.[1]

Adler answered them that what he had discovered was
not new; it was as old as the religions of the world. Nevertheless, it was what the world needed, and it could be
summed up in the ancient commandment: "Thou shalt love
thy neighbor as thyself."

After Adler's experience in World War I, he had come to
the clear conclusion that if man could not learn to practice
this principle, the world would destroy itself. Prior to the
war he had already seen the importance of "social interest"
or the individual's concern for the common good, but after
the war he felt it was the one hope for mankind.

Adler's most productive years were to follow. He began
to apply his principle in the treatment of emotionally disturbed patients who had not responded to other approaches,
and large numbers of them recovered. Among these people,
a high percent were depressed, and their depression ended.

Many of these difficulties, said Adler, arose from egocentricity. This egocentricity is an attempt of the individual
to isolate himself, and a lust for power over others accompanies isolation. This person is immature and expects the
world to revolve around him. The antidote is to "break up
the egocentric goal." One must begin to think of the common good and to behave accordingly.

Isolation and unrealistic demands are counteracted as the
person begins to serve others. To put it in everyday words,
one begins to live more unselfishly, and as he does so, he
bridges the gap between himself and others.

Whether the basic formulations of all of Adler's theories were right is no particular problem here. The practical point is that the application of re-education for altruistic service seemed to work with a large number of people, giving them an easily understood way of achieving greater happiness.

As Adler said, there was nothing new in his method. For centuries people have observed that the happiest people were those who were considerate of others, and who spent their energies for the welfare of others.

The Adler System Works

Adler was confident that he could help adults change from egocentricity to social interest, and from depression to optimistic living. He felt also that children could be educated to this way of life until altruism became as natural to them "as breathing or the upright gait." He lived to see many of the school teachers of Vienna so fired with his ideas that they put them into practice in the classroom; and Adler witnessed the demonstration of their successes; and the authorities of Vienna testified that the impact of Adler's teaching upon the city had reduced the rate of juvenile delinquency.

A friend of mine who is a practicing psychotherapist was trying to help a depressed patient. He closed one conference by saying, "I would like for you to try an experiment for just one day. Tomorrow I want you to wake up with the determination to think as little of yourself as possible all day long. I want you to start the day by saying the thing and doing the thing that will make your family the happiest. When you go to work, think of what you can do on the job to help your fellow-workers and the other people you deal with. Try this for just one day and see what it will do for you, and inform me of the results next week."

After working hours the next day, the psychologist answered the doorbell and there was his patient, all smiles. "I couldn't wait until next week to report. This has been the happiest day I have ever lived. I have never felt better. I am all optimism. I know now I'm going to get well and I know how I'm going to do it!"

What is Unselfishness?

The cynic might object that there is no such thing as unselfishness, that the person who serves does it because he is rewarded. His reward may be a feeling of satisfaction or of happiness, but still he serves because of himself and what he gets out of it.

Part of the problem here is one of definition. Selfishness may be defined as an undue interest in self to the disregard of the welfare of others. Unselfishness would not, then, mean that the individual would have no thought, no regard, for himself. It would mean he would not have undue regard for himself and a disregard of others. The unselfish person may be defined as one who has due regard for others as well as himself.

The ancient commandment is worth analyzing: "Thou

shalt love thy neighbor as thyself." One is commanded to love his neighbor, but the measuring-rod for that love is the way he regards himself.

Of course the altruistic person works for the common good because of a reward. Many times this is an inner reward and is well deserved. It may be the reward of joy, or it may be a feeling of self-respect, a feeling of being worth something to others. We all need that feeling. Without it we are lost. Anton Boisen, noted author and a leader in the movement of pastoral psychiatry, in describing the mental illness that beset him, said that one of the reasons for his illness was a "catastrophic loss of self-respect." Without this knowledge of our worth to others we become ill and despondent. One of the causes of the blues is a feeling of worthlessness.

When you contribute to others in whatever way you can according to your capacity, you gain a feeling of worth. This feeling of worth counteracts the blues. You feel wanted. You know you are of some value to others. This gives you a good feeling, and this good feeling is a part of your emotional and mental well-being.

There are a number of good results from "social interest." You set up communication with others. A tie is established. This tie can be strengthened and broadened to include many people who are your friends. As communication becomes better, understanding of self and others grows more complete. A feeling of community develops. You are a part of a group, and the others in the group are a part of you. As this goes on the members of the friendly group have a growing sense of well-being.

Examples of How it Works

Harold Sherman, in his stimulating book, *How to Turn Failure Into Success*, gives the case of Jess Smith, who as a young man, became a door-to-door drug salesman.² After trying for eight days to sell drugs, and selling none, he became so despondent that he reported back to his boss that he was quitting the job because he was a failure as a salesman.

His boss refused to let him quit so Jess continued. He then began listening to the people who were his prospects. He found they needed some understanding person to talk to. They had troubles—physical troubles and other personal troubles. As Jess Smith learned to serve his clients, he began doing better and better on the job and later became a partner in a large drug manufacturing company. It was through service that he turned defeat into victory, and pessimism into optimism.

Jess Smith is just one among many thousands who have discovered this practical, simple, but valuable method of beating the blues. What a wonderful world we would have if the majority of human beings could catch this vision and live by it. Alfred Adler's impact on the city of Vienna was one of the most remarkable achievements of this century. A city was beginning to be transformed by this ideal which Adler passionately believed in and practiced. The process was interrupted by Hitler, who represents the antithesis: egocentricity, hatred, the lust for power, disregard for the welfare of others.

A number of years ago many of us were inspired by the unusual account of a transformation that took place in the life of Vash Young, who was one of the outstanding life insurance salesmen of his generation.[3] Vash Young wrote his story and it was read by multitudes. He told it over and over again on the lecture platform to a great variety of audiences.

He had been an advertising salesman of moderate success financially. As a person he considered himself a failure. He was a failure because his life had been built on fear. As a fearful person he was pessimistic, irritable, constantly worried about business, indecisive, envious of others.

Part of his beginning a new life was to quit his old job with its financial security, to the alarm of his friends. He began a new type of work entirely on a commission basis with less than a hundred dollars in cash on hand and a wife and daughter to care for.

He began on his own a program of positive thinking. Whenever pessimistic thoughts and feelings tried to take over, Vash Young began consciously to substitute optimistic, courageous thoughts and feelings in their place. He had determined to divorce himself from fear and pessimism and to live by faith and courage. He had found that fear produced only unhappiness, and he had made up his mind to be done with it.

The result was that he became a "confirmed optimist, the most gullible man in the world, believing all the good things said about life."

He reported that he stopped thinking about himself and began to think of others instead. He made a rule that if anyone needed help, he would heed this call before a business call. He did this repeatedly. To most businessmen this would have seemed the way of folly, but Vash Young never regretted this policy. The inner dividends of happiness were great and he found that even financially he was far better off than he had ever been.

He wrote that one of his former troubles had been the "getting habit." He substituted for this the "giving habit."

As he began to analyze himself, he used the analogy of a factory. "Suppose you owned a factory," I said to myself, "would you manufacture only stuff that you do not want, do not need, and cannot use to advantage? You do own a factory, a thought factory . . . and you have turned it into a producer of junk . . . Fear, worry, impatience, anger, doubt. . . . Your factory is a menace to yourself and a nuisance to others." [4]

He reported that for a time after his change his household was "hard up" but happier than they had ever been. He was fighting a battle to "get rid of self-centeredness" and was winning. This, of course, is the Adlerian method.

His financial condition became desperate and he found himself about to slip back into his old ways of thinking and feeling. But he told himself, "When you are keenly conscious of your own needs, go out and do something for somebody else." So he volunteered to entertain the children at a hospital for crippled children. Each Sunday for an entire year he entertained these children.

Vash Young's recipe for depression-free, optimistic living is quite simple. Substitute positive thoughts and feelings for the negative. Live a life of service for others. It worked for him in every area of his life.

Particularly this second principle was what Alfred Adler believed was the hope for mankind. This, of course, is an oversimplification of Adlerian psychology, but this was the essence of his therapy. Adler took depressed people, found their unique "style of life," and re-educated them to use their unique abilities in service to others.

This is something that you and I can do. It is the sort of thing that pays the biggest dividends to us and to the society in which we live. Adler felt that as a person started living for the common good, his entire environment began cooperating with him to give him a fuller, more satisfying life. Many who have walked this road can attest that this is true.

---

[1] Bottome, Phyllis. *Alfred Adler*. New York: The Vanguard Press, 1957, pp. 120-133.

[2] Sherman, Harold. *How to Turn Failure Into Success*. Englewood Cliffs, New Jersey: Prentice-Hall, 1958, p. 36.

[3] Young, Vashni. *A Fortune to Share*. New York: The Bobbs-Merrill Company, 1931.

[4] *Ibid.*, pp. 46-47.

CHAPTER 4.

You Can Talk Yourself Out of the Blues

FOR A HIGH PERCENTAGE of people this method is highly successful. It seems that even animals get release from emotions by vocalizing them. And about the only way an infant has of expressing his troublesome emotions is vocally.

This early vocal release of emotions may well be part of the reason why in adult life, the individual gets release from talking it out. There are other reasons as well.

Not long ago in this area, a jet plane crashed, killing several people. There were also a few survivors, some of whom had injuries and were hospitalized. It was noticed that these survivors told and re-told the entire story of the plane crash. There was an emotional pressure from fear, excitement, and gratitude for being alive that seemed to compel them to repeat their story in detail again and again. This reaction has been observed after disasters many times.

Quite a few people have also had the following experience while sitting next to a complete stranger on a train, bus, plane, or ship. On short acquaintance one's companion will begin to talk about his most intimate affairs—problems, sorrows, and worries. There is a great inner need in most of us to talk out our difficulties with someone who will listen with some show of understanding.

The probability of this method of "talking it out" helping you is great. The person who is not helped is very much the exception. There are some guidelines about talking it out that may not only be helpful but necessary before you get the most benefit from the method.

The World's Religions and Confession

There is a long history of people being helped by verbalizing their troubles. Every major religion of the world has advocated confession. Sometimes this was for harsh theological reasons, which might seem neither acceptable nor reasonable to many people. The point is that in these major religions it has been discovered that usually the person feels relieved and unburdened after he has made his confession. Perhaps without consciously aiming at it, the confessional has frequently contributed to the mental health of the people who availed themselves of it.

One of the drawbacks of confession as used by some

churches is that as tensions are relieved, others are created. Normal types of behavior may be branded as sinful. Small misdeeds are magnified and guilt develops about something which is not really significant. There are tensions enough in life without needlessly manufacturing more.

Certainly every person should develop a sense of guilt, particularly about mistreating others. But this is quite different from the guilt that results when some religious bodies teach that small harmless acts are sinful. This, of course, is not true of all churches.

Sigmund Freud's Free-association

Sigmund Freud was the great pioneer who blazed a trail for those investigating the problems of mental and emotional disturbances of all kinds. Early in his treatment of neurotic people, Freud used the method that he called "free-association." The patient was instructed to talk freely about himself and his troubles.[1] He was instructed to say anything that came into his mind and to express his feelings completely and spontaneously. The therapist took note of this material, studied it carefully, and came up with interpretations that helped the patient understand his difficulty.

But one of the facts that soon stood out was that this free self-expression gave the person a wonderful sense of relief. Freud called it "catharsis," which meant a cleansing or purging.

Most of the other great pioneers in dealing with people's

troubles used this "talking-it-out" method and found the same result that Freud and the world's religions had found. Carl G. Jung, the eminent Swiss psychiatrist, who later came to America, found the same benefits of relief in his patients after they had verbalized their troubles. Alfred Adler, discussed in the previous chapter, also used this method to help lift the emotional burden of his patients.

Since the time of these three great explorers in the fields of mental health, thousands of psychotherapists have corroborated their findings as to the benefits of giving free verbal expression to emotion and using spontaneous speech to clarify problems. Dr. L. R. Wolberg, professor of psychiatry at New York Medical College, has an interesting comment to make on this subject.

> "Confession," "talking things out" and "getting things off one's chest," in relation to a friend or a professional person, such as a physician, minister or teacher, are common methods of relieving emotional tension. Beneficial effects are due to the release of pent-up feelings and emotions and the subjection of inner painful elements to objective reappraisal. The mere verbalization of aspects of the self of which the individual is ashamed or fearful helps him to develop a more constructive attitude toward them.
>
> Ventilation by the person of his fears, hopes, ambitions and demands often gives him relief, particularly when his verbalizations are subjected to the uncritical and sympathetic appraisal of the listener. Hitherto, the patient has covered up memories, conflicts and impulses that he has dared not admit to himself, let

alone others. A growing confidence in the therapist makes him feel that he has an ally who will help him bear fearful inner secrets. The ability to share his troubles with a sympathetic and understanding person robs them of their frightening quality. In addition, the patient may find that his judgment as to the viciousness of his experiences is distorted. The very act of translating inner feelings into words helps to restore mastery. The fact that he has not been rejected by the therapist, even though he has revealed his shortcomings, encourages him to reexamine himself.[2]

Industry Has Discovered the Good of Talking it Out

The story of how the Hawthorne Plant of Western Electric Company discovered the morale-boosting value of the talking-it-out method is a long and fascinating one.[3]

The company had promoted an extensive research program to discover how they could increase the production of their workers. They experimented with how work areas were lighted with no positive results. They kept records of the kind and amount of food the workers ate, and the temperature and humidity of the workrooms. They gave workers periodic medical examinations. Records were kept of how long the workers slept. This was done for a period of five years.

Results? Next to nothing! Finally the investigators came to one major conclusion: The factor that really counted in production was morale. The investigators then began an extensive program of what they called "interviewing." These interviews were conducted according to certain basic guidelines. The interviewer gave no advice, nor made moral judgments. He did not argue or try to be clever or dominate the conversation. No leading questions were asked. The interviewer merely tried to be a good, sympathetic listener.

With this approach they found the workers would tell freely what they were feeling and thinking. They were frank about their complaints. But they wanted also to talk about their personal problems away from work, marital and family problems, or troubles dating back many years.

The investigators discovered that frequently just talking about the problems made them disappear. For example, one woman worker complained bitterly about the poor food being served in the company dining room. Later she met the interviewer and thanked him for getting into action and improving the food.

But nothing had been done at all! The improvement was all in the woman's attitude, changed by talking it out.

The benefits of interviewing began to show up by greatly increased production, and also in the relations of the workers with each other. There was a general rise in morale.

The company then began a program of counseling. The counselors selected were just friendly company people who could listen sympathetically to fellow-workers and who could keep a confidence. What the workers needed to better their attitudes was a chance to talk about their troubles to an understanding listener. And in this case these listening-counselors were in no sense professionally trained people.

The benefits of this new point of view and different method spread widely. Supervisors and others in positions of management were oriented toward the attitude of listening as workers talked about their problems on and off the job. The workers' feelings, reactions, and ideas became a matter of major importance. Morale all over the plant was appreciably improved.

Carl Roger's Client-centered Approach

A very contemporary figure in the field of mental health, Dr. Carl Ransom Rogers, has greatly emphasized the dividends coming from the "talking it out" method. Dr. Rogers advocates what he calls "client-centered therapy" in which the person coming for help begins to talk about his problems or anything that worries him.[4] The counselor does not give him advice, neither does he diagnose the person's trouble. What the counselor does is to provide the troubled person with an atmosphere of complete acceptance and understanding, in which any and all of his emotional difficulties can be ventilated. In such an atmosphere, with the unconditional regard of the counselor to help him feel secure, the "clent," as the counseled person is called, feels freer and freer to explore his own feelings and put them into words.

What Dr. Rogers and a great host of counselors and psychotherapists who follow his principles have found out is that not only do people get catharsis for their negative emotions, but as they are relieved of these stresses they begin to develop more and more insight into their problems. They begin to experience more positive emotions. Positive attitudes begin to appear. Clients develop more understanding of how to solve their problems and usually go into programs of constructive action toward solving their problems.

You Can Get Help From Talking It Out With Nonprofessional People

Perhaps now you are thinking, "This all sounds very fine. But these troubled people all went to a trained counselor or a psychotherapist for help. I don't think my trouble warrants going to a psychotherapist. Yes, I'm having problems, but everybody does. Can I get help this way without going to a professional psychotherapist, and if so, how?"

Yes, you certainly can get help this way without going to a professional. You can find someone you trust and confide in this person fully and freely. In Dr. Wolberg's text quoted above, in addition to mentioning professionals, he says also that you may get benefit from talking it out with a friend. Also, the industrial counseling program mentioned earlier used sympathetic, friendly people without professional training.

A few words of caution should be given. Find someone who can keep a confidence. This person is not always easy to find, but he can be found. In fact, everyone who does not have a friend of this kind should search until he has found one. Life is not as rich and full as it should be until you have such a friend.

I know three interesting people who had a successful system. They made a pact with each other. Whenever any one of the three is depressed or worried he may feel free to call on either of the other two who is available. He knows he can get an understanding ear. He knows he is not going to hear any preaching or get a lot of phoney advice. This has been of untold value to each of these three individuals.

When you find a person in whom you can confide, it might be well to tell him that you do not need advice; you only want someone to talk to who will listen with understanding while you express your feelings freely in his presence.

Sometimes this individual may be your neighbor or a schoolteacher or someone you work with. Sometimes a pastor is the one you are looking for. In each case quite a few preliminary contacts would show you whether this is the listener you can talk to and upon whom you can rely.

The Ideas of the Semanticists

An interesting point of view having to do with personality disturbances, and emotional difficulties comes from a school of thought which emphasizes the role of language and speech in mental health. The professionals in this school of thought, called the Semanticists, are well represented by Dr. Wendell Johnson, an authority on speech problems, speech therapy, and psychotherapy as it is related to speech.

Dr. Johnson has written a significant book, *People in Quandaries*, in which he quotes psychiatrist Dr. Coyn Campbell.[5] Dr. Campbell stated that, in working with disturbed people, if they can be led to express their troubles clearly, those troubles almost always tend to disappear. Conflicts expressed in this way, fully described, are more easily understood and then solutions are found. Dr. Rogers, whose client-centered therapy was discussed above, says virtually the same thing. He affirms that much in human experience has been ignored or, because of fear, has been suppressed and has never been symbolized in words. As a person symbolizes these experiences in speech they grow less troublesome and can be dealt with more realistically.

Taking a cue from these two authorities, when you begin to talk over your problems with someone else, go into as much detail about everything as you can. Express as clearly as possible just how you feel and just how you are affected. Put all your emotions into words. Try to verbalize as accurately as possible your frustrations, your feelings of defeat, your disappointments, your anger, and your sorrows. Get all of it off your chest.

Tell as fully as possible what you think lies behind your depressions or other troubles. Why do the blues strike you and what are their effects on you?

You Have Innate Forces for Growth

Dr. Carl Rogers is optimistic about human beings. Within each person, he says, are natural "forces for growth."[6] If the person is placed in a favorable environment, these forces for growth begin to assert themselves. The reason growth has not taken place is because the environment prevented it. Part of your needed favorable environment is an accepting, permissive relationship with another person, with whom you feel completely free to explore all your feelings, your thoughts, your values, your motives, your aims. As you explore these, as you talk freely in this atmosphere of acceptance and understanding, the negative aspects of personality begin to diminish. If you keep working at it you may be completely released from them. Your natural forces for growth begin to make themselves known more and more. You come to recognize these positive forces and to encourage them, and they lead you to begin a new life of more positive living.

---

[1] Fine, Reuben. *Freud, A Critical Re-evaluation of this Theories.* New York: David McKay, 1964, pp. 16-19.

[2] Wolberg, Lewis R. *The Technique of Psychotherapy.* New York: Grune & Stratton, 1967, p. 87.

[3] Roethlisberger, F. J. *Management and Morale.* Cambridge, Mass.: Harvard University Press, 1959, pp. 5-26.

[4] Rogers, Carl Ransom. *On Becoming a Person.* Boston: Houghton-Mifflin, p. 63.

[5] Johnson, Wendell. *People in Quandaries.* New York: Harper & Brothers, 1946, pp. 15-17.

[6] Rogers, Carl Ransom. *Client-centered Therapy.* Boston: Houghton-Mifflin, 1951, p. 147.

CHAPTER 5.

You Can Analyze Yourself

DR. LOUIS E. BISCH, former president of the American Medical Association, has an entire chapter of a book dedicated to the question "Why Did You Think You Needed a Psychiatrist?" [1] In this chapter he assumes that a number of his readers have had this in mind and he proceeds to show that many of the problems that drive people to seek psychiatric help are very much the problems of normal people.

Dr. Bisch later follows this with a chapter entitled "Conditions You Should Not Try to Cure Yourself." There are people with various physical or emotional disturbances who should seek expert professional help. But Dr. Bisch is right. The majority of people with problems do not need a psychiatrist. As far back as we have any record of the human race, man has been upset by problems of all kinds. He has been able usually to resolve these problems, and in working out solutions he has developed strength and resourcefulness.

There is a great deal you can find out about yourself if you set about it systematically. If you are periodically bothered by the blues or by worries, the more you know about yourself, the better are your chances of improvement.

There are some precautions that should be given about self-analysis. It requires introspection which in itself may be either positive or negative. In excess, introspection may become negative. In order to avoid excess, it might be well to set aside a brief time each day to be devoted to self-analysis.

To counteract the possible negative effects of introspection, you can engage in activities that are social. The Adlerian emphasis in Chapter 3 on altruistic social interest would definitely tend to offset a tendency to become too wrapped up in yourself.

Dr. Karen Horney on Self-analysis

Perhaps it would be reassuring to you to know how certain authorities in the medical profession feel about self-analysis. For a number of years one of the leaders in psychiatry in the United States (she had practiced in Europe, too) was the late Dr. Karen Horney, who wrote a book called *Self-Analysis*.[2] One of her reasons for writing it was because of a shortage of psychiatrists. This shortage still exists. She felt that many people who had personality prob-

lems, even rather serious ones, could greatly better themselves through self-analysis.

She asks the question, "Can one recognize himself?"
meaning, of course, "Can he come to understand and know
himself?"[3] Her answer is that "people have always regarded
this task, though difficult, as feasible." Her goal in writing
about the subject was to help the person free himself from
inner bondages and liberate himself for a realization of his
capacities. Expressing it another way she would hope that
the person would get rid of his "phony self" and find his real
self.

One advantage in self-analysis, Dr. Horney points out, is
that while a therapist is with the client only about an hour,
the person undertaking self-analysis is with his analyst all
the time.

Her feeling that self-analysis is both desirable and feasible arose largely because of people she knew who had successfully achieved it.[4] As far as any dangers are concerned
she writes, ". . . in self-analysis the actual danger would be
less than in professional analysis."[5]

Dr. Horney presents what she calls "occasional self-
analysis," which she says is comparatively easy and sometimes brings betterment quickly.[6] An example she gives is
John, an amiable businessman, who had deep feelings of
inadequacy and suffered from headaches which apparently
had no physical cause.

John, his wife, and friends were going out for the eve-
ning. He wanted to go to one play but the others chose not
to follow his suggestion and outvoted him. During the play

the others chose, he developed a headache. In tracing back the events preceding the headache, he remembered that he had actually been quite angry at being overruled, while he had told himself he was being a good sport. When he recognized and admitted his anger, the headache was gone.

Following this, he had headaches three times, and each time he traced back until he found suppressed anger, at which point the headache would leave.

Dr. Horney also presents a longer case of a more detailed and complete systematic self-analysis.[7] She comments that this self-analysis is not a particularly brilliant one, that it is filled with blunders and deficiencies, but was nevertheless quite successful. Claire, the fictitious name of the young woman who analyzed herself, began recognizing certain emotional upsets and trying to find their real causes. Part of this had to do with her relationship with Peter, the man she wished to marry.

She began to record her dreams and made efforts to interpret them. She also began to note associations in her thought process. Some of these led her back to early childhood and her relationships with her mother. She also began to observe daydreams and fantasies and the associations they called up.

She kept notes of all her observations, associations, and interpretations. Frequently she studied these notes and wrote down her conclusions.

She came to see that her difficulty with Peter was because what she had mistaken for love was actually a neurotic dependency upon him. She was looking to him only for security. She expected gifts from him to symbolize this. She discovered she was really trying to exploit Peter, and this brought about a change in her attitude and behavior. She began to share his interests, think about his wishes. She began to give as well as receive.

However, Peter was a rather egocentric, unloving man. Gradually, she came to see him more clearly for what he really was. When he felt it was better for them to sever their relationship, she accepted his decision with calmness at first, followed by wild despair and finally by depression and suicidal ideas. She had experienced depression and suicidal ideas before, but this time, with great realism, she discarded all her suicidal ideas, admitting to herself that she really wanted to live and did not want to die. Following this, Claire developed clearer insights than ever into her compulsive dependency. Also she discovered that she had been afraid to live her own life in her own way. Her spells of misery began to diminish. She could see herself and her world more objectively.

To sum up Claire's results, her morbid dependency needs were broken. Her unhappiness was largely dispelled. Her periods of depression diminished. The interesting feature of all of this is that Claire successfully analyzed herself and increased her satisfactions in life.

All the way through Dr. Horney's volume are pointers and guides that will help you if you wish to arrive at a clearer understanding of yourself. If you are troubled with depressions, the probability is high that with intelligent effort, you might well find the basis of your difficulty and free yourself from it.

In the medical profession, is Dr. Horney alone in advocating self-analysis? Far from it. In the beginning of this chapter, Dr. Louis E. Bisch, past president of the conservative American Medical Association, was mentioned as writing a book along this line. His book is entitled *Cure Your Nerves Yourself*. Certainly Dr. Bisch is using "nerves" in the sense that the public uses it. The nerves themselves are not sick. When a person is emotionally and mentally disturbed, many times we say he has a case of "nerves."

Dr. Bisch states that ". . . if you think you need psychiatric advice don't rush to the psychiatrist until you are sure you cannot help yourself." [8] He further says that his book is written to "prove to you that most cases of nerves do not require professional psychiatric treatment," and "to show you how you can cure yourself."

He then follows with some very down-to-earth suggestions for emotionally disturbed people. For example, he has one chapter devoted to advice against being too self-centered. Another chapter discusses immaturity as the cause for much disturbance, and still a third treats the suffering resulting from an overactive conscience and an excess of guilt about small things.

To be sure, Dr. Bisch does not suggest systematic self-analysis as does Dr. Horney. But implied in every word that he writes is the desirability of your finding out your own trouble and doing something about it.

It has become increasingly clear that in the medical profession there are outstanding leaders who feel that self-help is practical and in many cases, all that is really needed. Another spokesman for this point of view is Dr. Camilla M.

Anderson, assistant professor of psychiatry at the Utah College of Medicine. She devotes space to self-analysis in her book, *Beyond Freud.*[9]

Dr. Anderson feels that the public has long had the mistaken idea that only deep analysis, delving into the unconscious, is effective, while there is nothing "either mystical or magical about discovering oneself."

The major difficulty is seeing and understanding those things about yourself that you have taken for granted. But, according to Dr. Anderson, your self-analysis can be successful. She outlines five ways to go about this.

1. Look for behavior patterns that repeat themselves.

2. Note your assumptions with regard to proper and improper behavior in both actor and reactor.

This point requires some explanation. Dr. Anderson believes that successful and satisfying living comes from behaving realistically in regard to every situation in which you find yourself. Certain "value-judgments" or assumptions that have previously been formed which do not apply in this situation keep a person from such realistic behavior.

An example of this would be the girl who has grown up with a father who grants her every whim, no matter how unreasonable. Her assumption is that the role of the male in the home is unquestioningly to grant every wish of the female.

When she marries, this assumption is unrealistic. She (the actor) gets unpleasant results from her husband (the reactor) when her assumption demands unquestioning subservience to her neurotic needs. Thus Dr. Anderson is suggesting that in self-analysis one needs to examine his assumptions in interpersonal relations to determine how realistic they are.

3. Discover what things are essential to your needs, understanding that the more essential it is, the stronger your feelings about it will be.

4. Pay special attention to the things in your life that threaten you, creating in you defensive emotions.

5. Take notice of your behavioral symptoms under threat.

And, says Dr. Anderson, keep asking the question "why" about everything you discover. You can find answers. An additional difficulty in self-analysis is that the interpersonal relationship of psychotherapy is missing. The therapist accepts you and believes in you. It becomes easier, then, to accept yourself. But eventually all you are learning must be applied outside of the therapist's shelter.

Analysis is not just a matter of discovering causes of symptoms, it is a matter of slow development. Part of this development is to suspend judgment of both others and yourself. Greater tolerance toward others and toward yourself is essential for beginning and continuing the growth process.

In such a way, Dr. Anderson recommends that you try self-analysis, with confidence that you will become your complete and whole self.

Basic to all healing is self-healing. Mechanical engineers foresee the day when many of our machines will be self-repairing. Living organisms to a great extent are self-repairing. Processes of repair can be aided, can sometimes be accelerated, but it is the healing forces within the organism which do the real work. Quite evidently, this applies not only to physical health but also to mental and emotional health.

Alfred Adler expressed this many years ago when he wrote that the actual change in the patient "can only be his own doing," and that "the responsibility for his cure is the patient's business." This also applied to the alleviation of symptoms, said Adler.[10]

Self-discovery and self-improvement are great adventures that await us all, and within all of us are those potentialities for growth which only need a chance to lead us to happier living.

1 Bisch, Louis E. *Cure Your Nerves Yourself*. Greenwich, Conn.: Fawcett Publications, 1961, p. 11.

2 Horney, Karen. *Self-Analysis*. New York: W. W. Norton & Company, 1947.

3 *Ibid.*, p. 17.

4 *Ibid.*, p. 28.

5 *Ibid.*, p. 33.

6 *Ibid.*, pp. 174-188.

7 *Ibid.*, pp. 191-192.

8 Bisch, Louis E. *Op. cit.*, p. 9.

9 Anderson, C. M. *Beyond Freud*. New York: Harper & Brothers, 1957, pp. 259-60.

10 Adler, Alfred. *Individual Psychology*. New York: Basic Books, 1959, p. 336.

CHAPTER 6.

You Can Write the Blues Out of Your System

You CAN USE WRITING to help you beat the blues. The major method of writing it out of your system that this author has used to help people help themselves is what I have chosen to call the "emotional autobiography."

Most school children at two or three points in their schooling are assigned the task of writing an autobiography. Usually this turns out to be a set of facts about the student's life. He writes when and where he was born, how many brothers and sisters he has. He writes about when he started to go to school and what his hobbies are. Perhaps he tells what business his father is in.

This type of autobiography is nearly worthless as far as helping with your emotions.

My instructions to people who decide to write their autobiography sound something like this:

Dramatize Your Emotions

"That you started to school in Jonesboro in September of 1935 is not the point at all. How did you *feel* about it? How did you react to your first teacher? What about your relations to the other students? Were you timid and self-conscious? Did someone tease you? Did you get angry?

"What happened that first day? How did you feel when your parents told you good-bye as they left you at the school? Or did your mother have to go in with you? When she left what did you do and how did you feel?

"It is not important to put down only that you were the oldest of five children. Do you remember when the next baby was born or the second? What were you feeling and thinking? How did you behave? What have been your relations with your brothers and sisters—jealousies, angers, rivalries, joys? It's getting your *feelings* down that does you the real good!"

One girl wrote "When I was in high school a friend and I went to see the movie *Dracula*. That was one of my most horrible experiences. I thought I would die of fright before the film was over. The scenes of terror kept running before my eyes when I walked in a daze away from the theater. My friend and I jumped and screamed at the slightest noise all the way home. For two months following, I still had not completely recovered from the shock of that experience."

A young man wrote, "I shall never forget when I was four years old how I felt when my father brought my mother and baby brother home. I had been sad and lonely for the week Mother was in the hospital. As the baby was put in his bed, Mother said to me 'Come look at your baby brother, Carl. Isn't he beautiful?' I looked at his red, wrinkled face and thought how ugly he looked. Mother said 'You must love him and be nice to him.' I didn't like him at all! I didn't like the way Mother looked at him. I resented it.

"Once Father caught me pinching the baby. He whipped me and scolded me and told me I was a hateful boy. He was right. I had begun to hate my brother. And I began to feel guilty when I felt hatred. This was the beginning of many years of deep resentment toward Father, Mother, and my brother. It was the beginning of troublesome guilt at the anger I felt toward this intruder who was stealing the affection and time of my mother away from me."

Two Benefits from the Autobiography

If you write your feelings down in this vein, it will usually do at least two things for you. First, you get it off your chest. Usually there is a feeling of great relief as you write down the things that upset you and about which you felt guilt. There is a catharsis or a purging effect.

Second, nearly always you will begin to understand yourself better. The young man mentioned above later in life developed periods of depression. Finding out about his deeply buried resentment toward his younger brother, and both his mother and father, and the accompanying feelings of guilt helped him to get rid of all these long-suppressed infantile feelings. His guilt feelings weakened and his depressions became less troublesome.

As you write in full about your past life you are reliving it. Reliving it makes you more objective and rational about it. The negative elements of the past begin to lose their grip on you. You are freeing yourself from the worst effects of the past.

One man wrote, "As the youngest child, and the only boy with three older sisters, I was pampered and spoiled and kept from maturing emotionally. I let my older sisters decide almost everything for me. Yet, as I became overdependent upon them, I also resented the decisions they made for me."

He went on to tell about instance after instance in which this pattern repeated itself as he grew up. When he married, he wanted his wife to decide things for him, but when she did, he became furious with her.

He felt badly about not being able to make his own decisions. He felt guilty about his outbursts of anger against his wife. He frequently found himself moody and pessimistic. Writing about it brought it all into perspective. He saw clearly the pattern of his life and what he must do to change it.

Most People Report Help from the Autobiography

Usually the person who writes this kind of autobiography will say that he has profited greatly by it. One man whose face comes easily to memory told me, "It was the turning point of my life. I saw why I was failing. My deep feelings of inadequacy were constantly telling me that I couldn't succeed at anything. And best of all, I found out where this too-low opinion of myself got started. It was back in that terrible neighborhood in Chicago where the other boys were always jeering at me and ridiculing me because of my nationality, my name, and my accent, all of them foreign to the neighborhood in which I lived."

The Diary Method

Many people find the writing of diaries helpful. Again you will profit most from a diary if you spell out in clear language how you feel about the happenings in your life. Writing the diary in this way can give you an emotional release and can also help you develop self-understanding. If you write an intellectual analysis of yourself it should usually be preceded by the chronicle of your emotional reactions.

One advantage of a diary that many people find is that they can look back over the years and see how problems were solved, how troubles usually dissipated, and how a process of growth took place. The person becomes more objective about himself.

Lincoln Wrote It Out of His System

I once read an anecdote about Abraham Lincoln that impressed me. Lincoln, then practicing law, had been wronged by another man. Abe sat in his office and wrote his angry response into a long letter, saying exactly how he felt in very plain language.

His law partner was surprised to see Abe tear the letter up and throw the scraps in the wastebasket. "Abe," he said "here you have spent all this time writing the letter and didn't even mail it. You wasted your time and energy."

"No," replied Abe, "I wrote my anger out of my system. Now I am better off for the writing and he is no worse off."

If this anecdote is true, Lincoln had learned the effective method of writing negative disturbances out of his system.

One man I knew told me that if he was disturbed, if he could sit down calmly and write what the disturbance was and what had caused it, he always felt better.

Preparing a Check-list Might Help

People who face the day with a feeling of depression because of the overwhelming number of tasks they face many times find it helpful to write all these tasks down in a list, starting with the most pressing and important and checking the item off the list when it has been done.

One mother of a large family told me this was her recipe. She said something like this:

"As my family grew, I found myself nervous and distraught because there were so many calls on my time and energy. As I awakened each morning, it was with a sense of a burden too heavy for me to bear. I told my doctor about this and he suggested writing down everything that was to be done and scratching off the most essential things first. This system gave me a sense of order and organization and put down in definite form what I had to do. I could set about doing my jobs calmly and with a sense of achievement as I checked them off the list. If it was an unpleasant job, when I checked it off I took a heavy black pencil and with considerable feeling blacked it off the list."

In talking to members of Alcoholics Anonymous, I have been told by members of certain local chapters that it is recommended to new members that they write an autobiography to help them take a personal inventory.

You can see, then, that many people can literally "write it out of their systems." You might experiment with some form of writing to see if it brings you the help it has brought to other people.

CHAPTER 7.

You May Get Help from Rational Psychotherapy

THE SUGGESTIONS YOU WILL FIND in this chapter and the one following are in some ways quite alike. In other ways there are great differences. This chapter discusses approaches to personal problems in a completely secular context. The chapter after this one does the same thing but in the context of religion. Both approaches are intensely practical.

There are several authorities in the field of psychotherapy who emphasize specific ways you can control your thought processes in order to control both your emotion and behavior. The most practical and the easiest to follow, in my opinion, is the system of Rational Therapy, taught by Dr. Albert Ellis.[1]

Dr. Ellis writes of the application of his methods largely to the problems of people who are neurotic. Here we are considering its use on a do-it-yourself basis with people who have periods of depression who could hardly be called neurotic. Our hope would also be that any deeply disturbed person might also benefit from what he finds here.

Most inner human problems are based upon some sort of misdirection, excess, or imbalance of the emotions. Dr. Ellis' Rational Therapy spells out a method of correcting some of the irrational causes of disturbing emotions.

First you will be interested in knowing the reasoning which provides the foundation for the methods.

Your Emotions May Be Due in Part to Self-Talk

First, Dr. Ellis holds that man's psychological disturbances (such as depression) are in part the result of irrational thinking.[2] This does not mean that he concludes this is the *only* source of emotion, but he believes that in man it is the most troublesome. ". . . Emotion is caused and controlled in several major ways; and one of these ways is by thinking." [3]

And how is most of our thinking done? It is done through "self-talk" or "internalized sentences." So a great deal of human emotion is caused by and sustained by self-talk.

The depressed person in his internalized sentences will most likely be saying, "This is a bad day. I am not doing well at all. Something is the matter with me. I can't do anything right. I should have stayed in bed this morning."

The optimistic person will probably be self-talking like this: "This is going to be a good day. I'm going to get a lot done today. I'm going to have the fun of seeing some people I like. It's good to be alive today. I am going to achieve some satisfying results today."

Through the thinking processes which take place chiefly through this self-talk, these two types of emotions are largely sustained.

Your Total Environment Influences Your Self-talk

As you develop, certain patterns of self-talk become habitual. What determines these patterns of self-talk? At first, the influences of the family have the greatest weight.

The little boy gets angry at his mother and shows it. His mother tells him, "You are a bad little boy to be angry with me. You should be ashamed of yourself. I am going to whip you for being angry with me."

This may be repeated many times in many ways. Eventually the child is telling himself, "I'm a bad boy. I do awful things. I feel terrible things. I think awful thoughts." He is well on his way to periods of depression because of guilt feelings.

Not only the family establishes patterns of defeating self-talk. From many sources in the environment you may have influences that tend to build up the destructive patterns. Neighbors and friends may add to it. The school may make its contribution.

You have only to read the newspapers to discover that most of the news deals with wars, death, destruction, sadness, accident, divorce, crime—generally a tidal-wave of descriptions of events that will add to your self-defeating, internalized sentences. Think also of the television programs that deal with death, destructive tension, and passionate uncontrolled emotions. Examine the fiction which is turned loose on the public. The largest amount of it again has to do with crime, seduction, rape, illicit love, extramarital sex adventures, stress, and excessive tension.

Is it any wonder, then, that so much of our thinking and feeling is destructive? The wonder is that people are able to survive this flood of darkness that pounds in upon us from our world environment.

Of course there are other forces that also influence our thinking positively. There are educational television and radio programs. There are creative teachers in the schools. Some newspapers try hard to magnify the positive side of the news. The *Christian Science Monitor* is, in the author's opinion, outstanding in its achievement along the lines of creative journalism. These positive forces are too few, but without them we would be in a hopeless situation.

Steps You Can Take to Change Negative Self-Talk

The first step toward correcting periods of depression, then, would be to become aware of negative patterns of self-talk. The second step would be to understand how these negative patterns of self-talk are disrupting life. The third step is to "re-think, challenge, contradict, and reverbalize these (and other similar sentences) so that . . . internalized thoughts become more logical and efficient."[4]

Irrational Ideas Sustain Negative Emotions

In his writings, Dr. Ellis names certain generally held irrational ideas that result in negative self-talk.[5] One of these is the idea that you must win everyone's love and approval. This is not only impossible in even a physical sense, but undesirable. If some people approved of you it would be a sign that something is radically wrong with your behavior, because some people have very poor standards of behavior by which they judge others.

Such an irrational idea would make you feel very inferior and even guilty every time anyone disapproved of you. Actually, the disapproval of some people might be the greatest compliment they could pay you.

If your life is governed by this irrational idea, your self-talk could become negative and damaging. Let us say you are faced with a simple choice of a candidate in a presidential election. You decide this on the best evidence you have and cast your vote for the candidate you conclude will be best for the nation.

Later you discover that very few people in your community voted your way. Your friends (if you divulge the way you voted) disapprove of your vote and bluntly tell you so. For days you go around feeling terrible because of their disapproval. You tell yourself, "Something must be wrong with me if I go against the majority. I have ruined myself with my friends, etc., etc."

Instead why not say to yourself, "I made the best choice I could with the information I had. I am proud that I can think and decide for myself rather than letting the approval or disapproval of my friends and family determine my choices and my actions."

There is a second irrational idea that many people hold and around which much defeating, discouraging self-talk takes place. To put this in my own words, Dr. Ellis' general idea is that many of us feel that in order to have any self-respect or respect from others, everything we do must be done perfectly or very nearly so. Ellis says that no one "can be perfectly competent and masterful in all or most respects." [6] Surely one tries to succeed, but to demand of himself perfection is to create anxiety and feelings of worthlessness.

So the self-talk of such a person might be, "I made a boo-boo. I made a fool of myself. Why am I always blundering and making myself ridiculous before others? I'll never try that again."

Enjoy the process of doing, says Ellis, rather than kill yourself trying to perform perfectly. If you want to do well, you should accept errors and blunders as part of the learning process.

I know many people who cheat themselves out of a great many good times because they are constantly fearful of making mistakes, or extremely worried about how they are going to look to other people.

Dr. Ellis' irrational idea number five is that the individual believes that "unhappiness is externally caused" and that he has little or no control over his "sorrows and disturbances."

Most of the time, it is our own attitudes which are responsible for our unhappiness. These attitudes are largely maintained by internalized sentences such as, "I always get the bad breaks. People are always taking advantage of me. I am terribly hurt because my friend slighted me."

Instead we could just as well say to ourselves, "I'll get my share of the good breaks. When the bad breaks come I'll know how to get around them. I'll be more alert in the future so people can't take advantage of me. If my friend slighted me, maybe he was worried or something. If he continues to slight me, I can find friends who will return my friendship."

The fact is that we have in us the power to control the way almost any situation affects us. We can make ourselves perpetually miserable or consistently happy, whichever we choose.

Dr. Ellis indicates another area of irrationality. If something is dangerous or threatening, we sometimes feel we should keep thinking about it and the probability of its happening. He says that to think in advance about something dangerous *in order to prevent it* is practical, but so many times all we are doing is entertaining a nagging dread that has nothing to do with averting danger. Rather this worry prevents the clear thinking that might lead to avoiding trouble. What kind of self-talk would tend to perpetuate this type of anxiety?

The person would probably have internalized sentences something like this: "When I start on this trip something terrible might happen to me. There are so many accidents today. I am almost bound to become the victim of one. I oughtn't to make this trip. It's too dangerous. Oh, I wish I knew what to do! I want to go but I'm afraid to go."

Instead, if this is a trip that should be taken or if it is a visit that should be pleasurable and bring others pleasure why not this: "This trip will be a good one. I'm going to have a good time. I'm going to enjoy driving. I'm going to drive cautiously and skillfully. I'm going to drive defensively and watch the other fellow. I'm not going to let fear cheat me out of the pleasure of this trip. I'm going to be confident and cheerful."

Another area of irrational self-talk, thinking, and emotion pointed out by Dr. Ellis is the notion that it is "easier to avoid than face . . . difficulty . . . and responsibility." [7]

In the long-run it is best (just what do we mean by "easy"?) to face responsibility, solve our problems, do our work, and try to reach our objectives. We defraud ourselves by the habit of avoiding responsibility.

Again, let us see if we can imagine the self-talk of the person who is evading and avoiding: "Wish I didn't have to go to work today. It's going to be bad! So much effort. So many decisions to make. I'll probably do everything wrong. I'll be exhausted before I've been on the job two hours. It's terrible having to go through this grind day after day."

Would this be better? "I've got a hard job ahead of me today. I'll try to do it right. I'll be as pleasant as I can on the job and get along the best I can with everybody. I may make mistakes, but everybody does. I'll keep my mistakes to the minimum. I'm going to be confident and clear-headed."

Dr. Ellis' ninth point deals with the influence of the past upon our present and future conduct. Some people are slaves to their past.[8] Because things have been bad in the past, there is a conviction that they will always be bad. Because there has been failure in the past, there will always be failure. This attitude makes it easy for us to excuse our present inefficient, unsatisfactory way of living. But because these negative elements have governed us in the past does not mean that they need govern us now and in the future.

Yes, says Dr. Ellis, it is good to know that the past may continue to have some influence on our behavior, but by working at betterment right now we can make the future better as well as the present. We can begin to create a new past that will have a positive rather than a negative influence.

The negative self-talk might run something like this: "I've never been able to keep friends. I make friends and they lose interest in me. I suppose I'll always be a friendless, lonely person, finding someone I like only to have them reject me. I've been that way all my life and I'm doomed to go on that way."

Instead, why not: "Something's been wrong with my ex-
pectancies of people in the past. Why do I make friends
only to lose them? There's bound to be a reason and I'll find
it out. Maybe I cultivate people for a while and expect the
friendship to continue automatically. Maybe I need to work
at it harder. Friendship must be like a garden. You cultivate,
plant, and water. Things begin to grow. You still have to
work at it, take out weeds, kill bugs and keep the ground
cultivated. I'm going to keep my friends from now on!"

All told, Dr. Ellis describes eleven of these irrational
ideas to guide the individual in finding out what his negative and destructive patterns of self-talk are and how these
may be changed to positive, constructive patterns.

Scientific Evidence About the Influence of Words on Human Behavior

You may be asking the question, "Is there any real evidence that words affect our emotions? Is there any scientific
demonstration of this?"

This is a legitimate question. The answer to it is "Yes,
there is some scientific evidence that words affect our emotional states."

Before we take up the contribution of science toward
answering the question, let us examine it in the light of our
own experience.

Have you ever heard a pessimistic talk after which you
felt more pessimistic? The talk was only words. The only

thing that happened to you during the speech was that you listened to words.

On the other hand, a friend of mine was telling me of listening to a dynamic, optimistic person speak for an entire hour. My friend reported that the hour passed so quickly he was hardly aware of the passage of time. He said, "I was transported! When the speech was over, I was filled with confidence and joy. I felt I could reach my goals and really become somebody."

Again, why was he feeling so good? He only had been listening to words expressing thoughts. The words and the thoughts had affected his emotions and he was inspired, invigorated, and took a new lease on life.

Not only do words and thoughts affect our conscious feelings but they affect our other bodily processes. When you are hungry, begin to read descriptions of delicious food and notice how your mouth begins to water and perhaps you will even feel stomach contractions. But there is no food there, and not even a picture of food. There is no odor of food. There are only words, which are the symbols of food. The words alone start up the bodily processes.

On the strictly scientific side, the two experiments you will read briefly below have to do with conditioning involuntary bodily reactions to words, involving the effect of words upon the autonomic nervous system.

The first of these was performed by Dr. C. V. Hudgins a number of years ago at Clark University.[9] With rather complex apparatus and procedure, he conditioned human subjects so that when the experimenter said the word "contract," the pupil of the eye would contract. Normally the pupil contracts upon exposure to a bright light. Next he *whispered* the word "contract" with the subjects thinking the word at the same time. No light was turned on during the later tests.

Toward the end of the experiment the subjects could merely *think* the word and their pupils would contract!

A second similar experiment (by Dr. R. L. Roessler) was done by having subjects plunge their left hands into cold water.[10] Immediately the blood vessels of the surface of the hand contract voluntarily. The blood vessels of the *right* hand also contract. The amount of this contraction can be measured by a device called a plethysmograph. The experimenter says the word at the same time that the hand makes the cold plunge. Eventually the subjects could *think* the word and the blood vessels would contract.

Medical doctors in the field of psychosomatic medicine have been observing similar reactions involving thought, emotion, and health. Dr. Curt S. Wachtel, member of the New York Academy of Sciences, Fellow in Psychosomatic Medicine, and the New York Council of Surgeons, has written a book entitled *Your Mind Can Make You Sick or Well*.[11] You can see that Dr. Ellis has a great deal of evidence to support his idea that thoughts affect the emotions and that most of our thinking is made up of sentences or combinations of words. The emotions affect the functioning of our bodies in many ways including the occurrence of ill-health due to prolonged negative emotions or the end product of good health due to maintaining positive emotions and attitudes.

This does not mean that all poor health is due to negative emotions and all good health due to positive emotions. It means that as the person prolongs stressful emotions such as fear and anger, he becomes more vulnerable to illness. As he sustains positive emotions, he puts himself in a position which generally promotes good health.

Emotions are affected by thought and by language. Thought and language in turn affect the emotions. A measure of control or influence can be exerted upon our emotions by our patterns of thinking. In such a way, patterns of thinking at least in part determine the outcomes of our lives, health, achievement, and happiness. Dr. Ellis' system is well worth experimenting with.

Dr. Ellis on the Do-It-Yourself Approach

How does Dr. Ellis stand on the do-it-yourself approach to self-betterment? You can draw some accurate conclusions from the fact that Dr. Ellis collaborating with another experienced psychotherapist and writer, Dr. Robert A. Harper, has written an entire book as a guide for the person who is attempting self-improvement.

But to give the other side of the story, both of these authors feel that "self-analysis . . . has distinct limitations." [12] Many times the person reading directions for self-analysis completely misunderstands them. Of course, the authors are speaking in the main about people who are neurotic. But perhaps the same thing might hold for the individual who is not neurotic, but merely looking for ways of living more satisfactorily.

Having said that, however, Ellis and Harper point out that changes *do* come about from people reading books. Sometimes just reading and understanding one point may make a great deal of difference.

They illustrate the possibility of change by using an extreme case, more serious than neurosis, a psychotic (schizophrenic) man who had spent a year and a half in a state hospital and was released. He had experienced great difficulties in getting along with his own family. He did not communicate with his parents. He and his wife were close to divorce.

Then he read an article in which Dr. Ellis had said, "People and things are not in themselves upsetting. Rather it is our telling ourselves that they are upsetting which upsets us." [13] As a result of reading this and applying it to himself, Bob Smith (fictitious name) began to improve his relations with his parents, with his wife, and in general began relating to others better than he ever had before.

The authors then add, "So it *can* be done." They then cite numerous well-known examples from history of people who bettered themselves by clarifying their thinking. This was on a purely do-it-yourself basis.

They also point out that even a person who is getting psychotherapy from a professional is *not* going to be helped unless *he* is very active and persevering in self-analysis. Therapy is largely a matter of teaching the person to analyze himself.

This self-help book then proceeds to emphasize and elaborate some of the more practical aspects of rational therapy such as the influence of thinking (and self-talk) on our emotions, and overcoming the negative influences of the past. How to eradicate failure, overcome anxiety, and how to control your own destiny are parts of the sensible guidelines the authors give.

The authors disown any kinship with "positive thinking." However, their system has much in common with some of the techniques of positive thinking. There are some major differences too, as we shall see in the chapters that follow.

---

[1] Ellis, Albert. *Reason and Emotion in Psychotherapy*. New York: Lyle Stuart, 1962.

[2] *Ibid.*, p. 36.

[3] *Ibid.*, p. 41.

[4] *Ibid.*, p. 59.

[5] *Ibid.*, Chap. 3.

[6] *Ibid.*, p. 63.

[7] *Ibid.*, p. 78.

[8] *Ibid.*, p. 82.

[9] Hudgins, C. V. "Conditioning and the voluntary control of the pupillary reflex." *Journal of Genetic Psychology*, 8: 3-51, 1933.

[10] Roessler, R. L. and W. J. Brogden. "Conditioned differentiation of vasoconstriction to subvocal stimuli." *American Journal of Psychology*, 56:78-86, 1943.

[11] Wachtel, C. S. *Your Mind Can Make You Sick or Well*. New York: Prentice Hall, 1959.

[12] Ellis, Albert and Robert A. Harper. *A Guide to Rational Living*. Englewood Cliffs, N. J.: Prentice-Hall, p. 1.

[13] *Ibid.*, p. 4.

CHAPTER 8.

You May Get Help from the Positive Thinkers

IN MANY WAYS SIMILAR to Dr. Ellis' Rational Psychotherapy are the psychological principles taught and practiced by certain religious groups. How many people have been benefitted by these groups is difficult to estimate. The number probably runs into multiplied millions. The sale and use of their most widely read books certainly reaches some almost astronomical figure, showing that there is a very great need in the present world for what they offer.

Broadly speaking, these religious groups may fall under the classification of what is generally called New Thought. My primary interest in the following discussion is to give you what the beneficiaries of these groups feel are practical,

87

useable methods of self-improvement in almost every department of one's life. My emphasis, then, will be more on the methods of self-improvement that are taught by the New Thought groups than on their theological and philosophical principles.

But since their methods are so closely tied in with their theological and philosophical principles, it is practically impossible to discuss the methods without reference to the underlying principles and beliefs.

The organization which now has the largest following among the New Thought groups is the Unity School of Christianity.[1] For this reason the discussion here will be largely related to this organization, with brief discussions of other New Thought groups, and the ideas of certain religious leaders from some of the other older denominations who follow the practical principles of New Thought.

You Will Find Optimism

All of the New Thought groups are based upon the principle of unwavering, unconquerable, indestructible optimism. It is a fervor that runs through all their teachings. Their theology or theologies are optimistic. Their philosophy is optimistic. Their methods invariably carry with them the aura of optimism.

This may be one of the major reasons why they are so attractive to so many people. In a world where every newspaper (except those published by the New Thought groups) is predominantly the purveyor of bad news, where radio and T.V. are constantly blaring forth messages of flood, famine, disease, discord, crime, and above all war, the strong clear note of confidence, hope, and love sounded by the New Thought groups comes as a welcome, mind-healing contrast. In a world of upheaval and excessive stress, the individual is offered an inner world of peace and serenity. In a world of sickness and want, he is offered also the companionship of others who are in the process of creating their own wonderful inner worlds.

As an antidote to depression in the context of religion, the New Thought approach is most effective, as can be testified by thousands of adherents.

What are the practices that they advocate that produce such satisfying results?

Thinking is the Key

Primary importance is laid upon the process of thought. In one of Unity's approved books, the statement is made that "each of us is constantly making himself what he is. Unity reveals that our lives and affairs are completely influenced and shaped by the character of our thinking, that man is not limited by God's will or by heredity or environment or by fate or circumstance—but by his own dominant state of mind." [2] Or, to quote from another of Unity's approved books, "Every right thought that we think, our every unselfish word or action, is bound by immutable laws to be fraught with good results." [3]

What happens in one's life is largely the result, says Unity and other similar groups, of the thinking process. First comes the thought and as this thought persists, it is materialized and becomes substance. Think consistently the thoughts of health, and health will result. Develop the habit of creative thinking, and your life and its results will be creative. Think in terms of achievement, and you will achieve. Thought is the seed which becomes the substance of root, stem, leaves and finally the symmetrical flower of life. Likewise negative thinking results in negative living.

"You can't help thinking," says Mr. Butterworth, an author quoted above, "because you are a thinking being. You might as well learn to think right, and right thinking is prayer. Become a positive thinker and pray without ceasing." [4]

Thought processes determine your emotions, your health, and the outcome of all of your affairs. Right thinking or truth is the very presence of God. Thus thought processes are all-important in bringing about emotional and physical health, happiness, life's deepest satisfactions, and although this does *not* occupy a primary position of importance, material prosperity.

Thus you can control your thoughts and generally control the direction of your life. But what are the actual methods of control that are taught?

Affirmations and Denials

These fall broadly under two classifications. You must practice affirmations and denials if you are to control your thinking processes. As you come to understand this, you will begin to realize that Albert Ellis' system of psychotherapy follows (but only in part) the principles advocated by Unity but, as has been stated above, in a secular rather than a religious context. Of course, the principles of Unity date back to the 1890's, and Rational Psychotherapy is a fairly recent pronouncement.

Dr. H. E. Cady, perhaps the first to write a complete statement of the principles and practices of Unity, said, "Practice these denials and affirmations silently on the street, in the cars, when you are wakeful during the night, anywhere, everywhere, and they will give you a new . . . mastery over external things and over yourself." [5] She also says, [6] "The saying over and over of any denial or affirmation is a necessary training of a mind that has lived so long in error and false belief that it needs this constant repetition of Truth to unclothe it and clothe it anew." This is very much what Dr. Ellis echoes when he says that our culture has created in each of us negative "self-talk" that results in our living negative lives.

What does Unity mean by affirmations and denials?

"To affirm anything is to assert positively that it is so,

even in the face of all contrary evidence." That is, if things are not going well with you, begin to say that they will go well, that they *are* going well. Keep on asserting it and things will begin to change for the better.

To inject my own interpretation, here is what we have: Thought processes control life, and verbal processes control thought. Control your verbal processes and you master your thinking; master your thinking and you master your life.

The affirmations are stated in the language of religion as one would suppose. Although each individual may work out his own affirmations according to his own needs, the literature is filled with affirmations which will give him confidence and a sense of well-being.

The Power of Belief

It might be well to say here that belief of any kind is a powerful thing. Religious belief in which many of us have been nurtured since infancy has deep roots. If this is the case with you, if you can reasonably tie in your earlier beliefs with the morale-building methods of a number of religious groups, those methods may prove doubly effective.

The New Thought groups are strongly theistic. They believe that God is love, truth, life, law, beauty, goodness, peace, joy, abundance, and intelligence. They believe that God is universal mind. Everything is aimed at getting a man in harmony with these values that New Thought believes are the supreme values for mankind.

As the uninitiated read both the affirmations and denials written in the approved texts, he may be repelled by the unrealistic note they sound. If you feel sick, you are advised to think to yourself, "I *am* well," in order to get well. If you are afraid, it is recommended that you say, "I am not afraid. I *am* courageous."

I shall make no attempt here to defend this point of view. In each case the recommendation is made that you put the affirmation or denial in the present tense *as if* it were already true. Perhaps this statement of the *ideal* condition, the *desired* condition, is more effective in building confidence or morale.

Still, my own feeling from my knowledge of the flexibility of New Thought (and I have no authority for this but my own opinion) is that if you find repeating the affirmation of the ideal condition too extreme, a more moderate statement would be considered acceptable. If you are sick, then you would repeat, "I am going to get well" or "I'm not going to be sick for long."

But again, most of the literature suggests that affirming the ideal condition is therapeutic. Perhaps a certain amount of theology lies behind this. God is universal mind and man is made in the image of God. Man is potentially perfect. Man's essential nature is divine. Man should see himself as God sees him. As man sees himself in the light of God's thinking, idealistically, he grows more like God.

Denials Are to Correct Error

"Denials" are the undoing of wrong thoughts, beliefs, or feelings that have been implanted in you. An example of this is when the maturing child discovers there is really no "booger-man" or "bogey-man" which his unwise parents told him might "get him" if the child did not obey them. He says to himself, "There is no such thing." He has made a denial. He is freeing himself from a false idea.

If a statement is untrue, or a condition, such as want, is unnecessary, repeated denials of it, says New Thought, make the falsehood or condition lose its power over you. If a person had thought of himself as a failure, his denial would be "I am not a failure." His affirmation would be "I am successful." Repeating the denial and the affirmation would in time change the condition. A denial given in Dr. Cady's book to conquer fear is, "I am not afraid; I am perfect love and can know no fear. No one, nothing in all the universe can hurt me."

The Tolerance of New Thought Groups

Perhaps one of the appeals of the New Thought groups is their theological flexibility. As new truths are discovered, they should be appropriated. Discovery of truth is progressive and is going on all the time.

In the main they hold to the positive approach of Christianity, leaving out its negative elements. They have also incorporated some of the ideas of Oriental religions. There is really no hard and fast dogma or creed. There is great flexibility, and a relaxed tolerance toward all beliefs.

Other New Thought Organizations

While the discussion here has dealt principally with Unity, there are a number of other organized groups who hold essentially the same beliefs and advocate the same practices. One of these is called Religious Science.

The periodical which they publish is called *Science of Mind*, which not only carries inspirational articles on their teachings and methods, but from time to time publishes a scientific article by some outstanding or recognized scientist.

Another similar organization is Divine Science. Then there are perhaps a dozen or so that believe and practice essentially the same ideas and methods with minor differences and minor emphases.

The books and periodicals published by all these organizations have been widely circulated and read. Some of the writers with their ideas have not ever been officially members of any of the organizations.

One such writer was a man who lived to be ninety-two, whose name was amazingly Ralph Waldo Trine. His book *In Tune With the Infinite*, published in 1897, has continued to sell until now; the sales number in millions. A new edition published a few years ago vanished from the bookstores almost overnight—sold out.

The hard-headed realist will doubtless say, "Well, pain, poverty, and sickness are all here. They are real. We can see them and feel them. How can I bring myself to deny the reality of them?"

Error and Truth in Thought Processes

This point of view is easy to understand. The New Thought advocates say, "Why are these undesirable things here? Because man's error has brought them into being. Man has missed the mark of truth. These errors in man's thinking have created and perpetuated the undesirable conditions. To correct these errors we must begin to have new and different habits of thinking. You can begin to get rid of the undesirable in your own life by denials and affirmations that will eventually transform your life." And if enough people begin to deny poverty, sickness, and other undesirable conditions, and affirm abundance, health and desirable conditions, the world can literally be transformed because thought is followed by substance.

How effective are these morale-building religions? There is hardly any objective way of checking. There are, however, thousands of people who will testify that their lives have been immeasurably bettered by the practices they have learned from the New Thought approach.

The mind-over-matter thesis has been so widely discussed that it has become common knowledge. New Thought is doing an amazing job of demonstrating the thesis and translating the principle into the everyday lives of men and women in many places in the world.

You do not have to join their churches in order to learn their beliefs and to follow them.

---

[1] Braden, Charles S. *Spirits in Rebellion*. Dallas, Texas: Southern Methodist University Press, 1963, p. 235.

[2] Butterworth, Eric. *Unity, A Quest for Truth*. New York: Robert Speller and Sons, 1966, p. 44.

[3] Cady, H. E. *Lessons in Truth*. Lee's Summit, Missouri, 1966, p. 10.

[4] Butterworth, Eric. *Op. cit.*, p. 52.

[5] Cady, H. E. *Op. cit.*, p. 59.

[6] *Ibid.*, p. 53.

CHAPTER 9.

Leaders from Many Religions May Help You Think Positively

MANY OUTSTANDING RELIGIOUS LEADERS of various denominations have become infected with the New Thought principles and practices. As they have, their ministries seem to have become dynamic and far-reaching.

If you belong to any of several religious bodies, some of them with very old traditions, you can usually find a prominent spokesman for the New Thought ideology.

A Presbyterian Positive Thinker

For example, if you are a Presbyterian you might profit by the writings and the philosophy of the late Dr. Glenn

Clark, born and reared a Presbyterian, product of a Presbyterian college, and later a professor in a Presbyterian college.[1] He has exerted a vital influence in his own denomination, and through his encampments called The Camps Farthest Out, he has reached a multitude of people from all denominations. One of his books is *How to Find Health through Prayer* in which he advocates his own approach to denials and affirmations.[2]

In another book which went through at least a dozen editions, *The Soul's Sincere Desire,* Dr. Clark writes about the scriptural Psalms as effective denials and affirmations.[3] He uses the analogy of breathing to explain denials and affirmation. The affirmation is like breathing in fresh clean air with adequate oxygen. The denial is like the expulsion of air, getting rid of waste and poison. He follows this by giving examples of affirmations and denials. He uses the well-known Twenty-Third Psalm as a prime example. This Psalm has only two denials, but about ten or so affirmations. Dr. Clark lays great emphasis upon substituting constructive thoughts for destructive thoughts.

Another emphasis of Dr. Clark's is on the power of positive imagination. You can look at the way things are now, and imagine the way things could be and should be. While he advocates the repeated denials and affirmations, saying that the denials are protective and the affirmations are a venturing forth into the positive, at the same time he feels you may develop beyond denials and affirmations and use imagination instead. Here, of course, he is advocating that we *visualize* what we need and want, and want ourselves to become.

As with others we have discussed or will discuss, it is hard to estimate the number of people Dr. Clark has helped with his message of confidence, of optimism, and the value of deep religious experience.

I have talked with some who have attended the conferences or encampments that he calls The Camps Farthest Out. These people give evidence of the great personal benefits that accrue from contacts with Dr. Clark and his dynamic philosophy.

A Methodist Positive Thinker

If you are a Methodist, you might get help from the works of Dr. Lewis L. Dunnington, who has held important pastorates in Duluth and Iowa City.[4] During his pastorate at Duluth, he discovered on pastoral calls that his members were getting more real help from Unity publications than any other source. He paid a visit to Unity headquarters and was impressed to find Charles Fillmore, the Unity founder, in vigorous health at ninety years of age. In middle life he had been in poor health. Dunnington was impressed by the atmosphere of the large Unity establishment, the confidence and happiness of the sizeable force of people working there, and their remarkable teamwork. Here was a demonstration of practical Christianity that was truly effective in the lives of people.

This was the beginning of a transformation in Dr. Dunnington's ministry, as he testified. A change came over him and the congregation. The membership grew from about four hundred to over two thousand. His books multiplied his usefulness and sold widely.

In his book *The Inner Splendor,* you will find a chapter entitled "Health from Within." In it he says that one should pray for health. As you pray for health, you *visualize* your body radiant with health. By affirming that you have radiant health, you generate feelings of trust, harmonious living, and peace of mind. If you hold these affirmations in your thoughts persistently, the very cells of your body will be permeated with healing forces.[5]

Looking at the other side of the picture the author states that thoughts of fear and defeat negatively influence bodily functions. On the other hand, thoughts of faith and love send healing currents to the body cells.[6]

At the close of almost every chapter of this book and also others that he has written are the affirmations for the reader. In his book *Power to Become,* he has written that affirmations of abundance, health, love, and peace should be repeated until there is no room for destructive thoughts arising from hatred or hostility.[7]

A Positive Thinker From the Reformed Church

The influence of Dr. Norman Vincent Peale, a minister of the Reformed Church, is common knowledge. Latest reports show that his *Power of Positive Thinking* has sold over two million copies. His magazine *Guideposts,* with a wide circulation, carries in it, usually in the form of personal experiences, the same message as his several books.

If you read *The Power of Positive Thinking*, you will find that the author counsels his readers to repeat affirmations. Many times these are verses of scripture that strengthen faith in yourself and in God.

In the first chapter Dr. Peale tells of a man who came to him because of lack of confidence in himself. He was faced with an important business deal.

Dr. Peale told him he was going to give him "certain words" to repeat several times before going to sleep, before getting up, and again as he went to his appointments. His words were a well-known verse from the New Testament: "I can do all things through Christ which strengtheneth me." The man followed instructions and reported that his confidence was strengthened.

In the same chapter Dr. Peale tells of a traveling salesman who had morale-building verses of scripture in a clip on the instrument panel of his car. He said that while he was driving he had many thoughts and decided that he would eliminate the negative thoughts by having these helpful verses where he could commit them to memory.

Dr. Peale writes, "This plan used by my friend is a very wise one. By filling his mind with affirmations of the presence, support, and help of God, he had actually changed his thought processes. . . . We build up the feeling of insecurity or security by how we think. . . . And what is even more serious is the tendency to create, by the power of thought, the condition we fear. This salesman actually created positive results by vital thoughts of courage and confidence. . . ." [8]

Later he states that, "The words we speak have a direct and definite effect upon our thoughts. Thoughts create words, for words are the vehicles of ideas, but words also affect thoughts and help to condition if not to create attitudes." [9]

One of the differences between Dr. Peale and most of the New Thought literature is that Dr. Peale does not advocate the repetition of "denials" to help a person rid himself of undesirable attitudes. However, one of his chapters is entitled "I Don't Believe in Defeat." He also advocates repeating this sentence, but he calls it an affirmation. In the main, Dr. Peale seems to believe that affirmations are more effective than denials.

Elements of Positive Thinking from a Roman Catholic

From the Roman Catholic faith Ernest Dimnet writes a great deal having to do with positive thinking. In his book *The Art of Thinking,* he asks the question, "Can we think as we like?" [10] Then he goes on to say that we can choose our thoughts, and that for life to be lived at its best we should choose superior rather than mediocre lines of thinking. He emphasizes that attitude and actions of love liberate our higher levels of thinking. He says, "Do not read good books —life is too short for that—only read the best." While Abbe Dimnet's book was written primarily for writers, one can find in it elements of kinship with the positive thinkers.

I am not classifying Ernest Dimnet with the New Thought movement. But he exhibits many ideas similar to those of the positive thinkers. In his book *What We Live By*, he underscores the quest for beauty.[11] Many of the obstacles to self-improvement, he says, are in our minds. Man desires to improve and these desires are the basis for transformation. "An honest desire . . . is the foundation for all human action."

Images, he says, collect around them exceptional energy. "All depends on the power of the mental image." One of the first steps toward self-improvement is to pull aside from the mad, frantic, meaningless rush of life all around us.

He also recommends "an inventory of yourself." If we are to better ourselves, "the vision of our transformed self is the real motive power in our transformation." Then he writes that "we stand a better chance of becoming useful to our community if we optimistically visualize ourselves rivaling great reformers or philanthropists, than if the drooping image of our inadequacy is constantly before us." [12]

Part of self-betterment is a conscious and repeated period of meditation. "Meditation is a contented, but perfectly conscious, dwelling of the mind on something likely to elevate our life." [13]

One of the most important elements of self-improvement is true love, friendship, good-will. "True love makes our ideal brighter and our purpose stronger." [14]

This Roman Catholic author is mellow and optimistic. He gives you many sound and practical methods by which you can achieve genuine self-betterment. His ideas are quite close in many respects to the positive thinkers and the New

Thought groups. Of course, there also are some major differences.

A very early Catholic, St. Francis of Assisi, gives a recipe for positive thinking in one of his world-famous prayers:

SILENT COMMUNION FOR A
FAITH WITH POWER

O Lord make of me an instrument of Thy peace:
Where there is hatred let me put love,
Where there is resentment let me put forgiveness,
Where there is discord let me put unity,
Where there is doubt let me put faith,
Where there is error let me put truth,
Where there is despair let me bring happiness,
Where there is sadness let me bring joy,
Where there is darkness let me bring light.

O Master grant that I may desire rather:
To console than to be consoled,
To understand rather than to be understood,
To love rather than to be loved,
Because it is in giving that we receive;
In forgiving that we obtain forgiveness;
In dying that we rise to eternal life.

Positive Thinkers Who Are Episcopalians

If you have an Episcopalian background, you will find a number of its leaders and ministers whose teachings are in very close harmony with the New Thought philosophy and methods of combatting low morale and promoting strong morale.

The Rev. L. Douglas Gottschall of Oakland is not only rector of an Episcopal church, but also president of the College of Divine Science. The Rev. R. A. Russell in Denver, pastor of the Church of Epiphany, places emphasis in his writings upon the effectiveness of positive thinking in producing peace, love, joy, health, success, and many other benefits as contrasted with negative thinking which results in sorrow, misery, and failure.[15]

Positive Thinking From the World's Great Religions

You can easily see that many religious leaders have seen the practical benefits of affirmations, of denials, and of the verbal repetition of positive thoughts until they become strongly reinforced in your mind.

It seems to me that one could go through the scriptures of almost any of the world's living religions and glean from them enough affirmations so that the adherents of those religions could build confidence and high morale satisfactorily by frequently repeating such verses.

The great Mahatma Gandhi occasionally had periods of depression. His remedy for it was to read or to repeat comforting verses from the Hindu scriptures, after which he regained confidence and found his depression dispelled.

He said that when he could see no ray of hope, he would open the Bhagavad Gita and find a verse to comfort him. In the midst of sorrow, frustration, and disappointment, reading such an uplifting passage, he soon found he could smile again. He said that his life had been filled with tragedy and the fact that this had not affected him permanently was due to his use of the Bhagavad Gita to transform depression to confidence and courage.[16]

I might add a personal word here. I have respect for the personal religion of all people, although I might disagree with most. However, the majority of us are what we are in religion largely through teaching we received in childhood.

It seems to me that the course most of us ought to take is to hold on to whatever we can rationally from those original teachings. What we find negative and irrational we can discard. As we find help from other religious teachings, these we can assimilate into our personal philosophy.

This was the path of Mahatma Gandhi. He studied all religions. He acknowledged particularly the help that came to him from the Sermon on the Mount. He said, however, he could remain a Hindu and still incorporate the good from other religions into his life. Perhaps each of us could do something similar, appropriating what seems to be beautiful, good, and true from whatever sources they come, but keeping in mind that much of our early conditioning has deep roots from which can be cultivated a growth of rational, tolerant belief which will greatly benefit us as we seek happy, useful living.

---

[1] Braden, Chas. S. *Spirits in Rebellion*. Dallas, Texas: Southern Methodist University Press, 1963, p. 391.

[2] *Ibid.*, pp. 382-384.

[3] Clark, Glen. *The Soul's Sincere Desire*. Boston: Little, Brown, and Company, 1934, pp. 12-14.

[4] Braden, Chas., *Op. cit.*, pp. 381-382.

[5] Dunnington, L. L. *The Inner Splendor*. New York: The Macmillan Company, 1954, p. 42.

[6] *Ibid.*, p. 49.

[7] Dunnington, L. L. *Power to Become*.

[8] Peale, Norman Vincent. *The Power of Positive Thinking*. New York: Fawcett World Library, 1965, pp. 19-20.

[9] *Ibid.*, p. 33.

[10] Dimnet, Ernest. *The Art of Thinking*. New York: Simon and Schuster, 1932, pp. 116-129.

[11] Dimnet, Ernest. *What We Live By*. New York: Simon and Schuster, 1932.

[12] *Ibid.*, pp. 176-179.

[13] *Ibid.*, p. 194.

[14] *Ibid.*, p. 239.

[15] Russell, R. A. *You Can Get What You Want If You Return Home*. Denver, Colorado, 1948.

[16] Nanda, B. R. *Mahatma Gandhi: Biography*. Boston: Beacon Press, 1958, p. 70.

CHAPTER 10

The Business Blues:
Success Motivation Institute
Can Show You How
to Beat Them

Just to walk through the door of Success Motivation Institute means that you are on your way to beating the business blues. Here are the experts that can help you overhaul
yourself—a stem to stern job.

Contagious Optimism

Everyone in this Waco, Texas firm, from the custodians
to the dynamic president, Paul J. Meyer, are infected with

incurable, and, best of all, contagious optimism. It is catching and it is wonderful to know that the good things of life are catching.

A friend said to me once, "Yesterday started off bad. Later in the day I found things going well. I found myself confident, happy. I began to trace back during the day how the change had come about. Then I remembered: It was the smile of one person, spontaneous, radiant, friendly. That was when I began to feel good."

It is not only the smiles that greet you at SMI, it is the confidence, backed by an intelligent, proven system, that the morale of the individual, or of a small business, or of the largest corporation, can be improved. It is this confidence that is so infectious.

I knew a very young man who went to work part-time at SMI. In a few weeks he was steamed up so dramatically that I began to inquire what caused such a boost. This was my initial acquaintance with SMI. And this is the sort of thing they do for people, not only people in the business world, but anyone who needs to improve himself.

A Master Motivator

President Paul J. Meyer is many times called a master motivator. This is an accurate description of this man who before he reached the age of twenty-five had personally sold seven million dollars worth of ordinary life insurance within a period of thirty months. In twenty-four months he built an agency that produced thirty million dollars of ordinary insurance within a year. At the age of twenty-seven he became a millionaire. Now he is sharing his knowledge of self-motivation and the motivation of others with a multitude of people. SMI is the biggest business of its kind in the world.

W. Clement Stone, president of Combined Group of Insurance Companies, and editor and publisher of *Success Unlimited Magazine* wrote to Mr. Meyer, saying, "I like the way you write! I like the way you think! I admire your action! You certainly are the best in your field. You are destined to make Success Motivation Institute a force of great good for all people."

Help for the Small Businessman

What can SMI do for the small businessman who wishes to improve? The best way to answer this question is to let one of these small businessmen, who is no longer small, tell what happened to him.

MAN ATTRIBUTES SUCCESS IN BUSINESS
TO DYNAMICS OF SUPERVISION COURSE

Waco, Texas (UPI)—Two years ago, Arnold Huddleston ran a hamburger stand in nearby Temple, Texas. He couldn't work up enthusiasm for selling hamburgers and the company threatened to fire him.

But Huddleston couldn't quit. He had a wife and three children and needed the job. So he bought a set of phonograph records for which Dr. J. Clifton

Williams, Chairman of the Baylor University Psychology Department, wrote the script.

There was nothing on the records but a man reading what Williams had written. Huddleston listened faithfully and at the end of 60 days got a promotion instead of a dismissal.

He now manages the company's interest in Abilene, Texas. (The company owns hamburger shops in Temple, Abilene and Waco.) He makes $1,000-$1,100 a month, owns stock in the company and is on the board of directors.

The records to which Huddleston listened are the major part of a "DYNAMICS OF SUPERVISION" course which Williams prepared for Success Motivation Institute, Inc., of Waco, Texas.

The President of Success Motivation Institute is Paul Meyer, now 42, who had made a million dollars in insurance by the time he was 27 because he had an unusual talent for getting work done.

Trying to analyze the reasons people work hard, Meyer put incentive (money) and fear (threat of being fired) in the background. He got the idea that the way to make a person succeed in his work is to influence his thinking and attitude toward his job.

Meyer got Williams to prepare a course for supervisors with the idea of influencing attitude-toward-job. In addition to being a psychologist, Williams had worked as a management consultant.

The whole course is arranged so lessons are frequently reviewed.

"As soon as a man starts thinking like a supervisor, he is one," Williams says. "The secret is thought repetition. It's like a guy constantly hearing a particular tune on the radio. He soon starts humming it to himself without thinking.[1]

Williams denies that thought repetition through records could turn to sinister motive a person of normal morals, living in a normal environment. He says a person would be prevented by his own morals and background from being talked by record into anything wrong.

His records also tell supervisors that "you become successful as you help your company achieve its end.

"We try to build the thought that each person is a sort of little company himself, selling his services to the company he works for," he says.

Williams has a drawer full of testimonials, and, he says, a lot of people like Huddleston are ready to tell what "Dynamics of Supervision" has done for them.

Courses for Every Need and Every Pocketbook

SMI has courses suited to almost every pocketbook and almost every need. The smallest course is called "Blueprint for Success." While it is the shortest course, it is really a very large course, filled with dynamic morale-lifters. It is actually a six-week course, but the cost of it is very low.

The major course are planned for from fourteen to sixteen weeks. It is described as "a program designed to give direction to your dreams."

These courses are sold largely through more than five hundred distributors all over the world and are available in

French, German, Spanish, and Japanese. The courses have reached more than 250,000 people from 26,000 companies. Worldwide demand for the courses is constantly increasing.

Much of the advertising for these courses is by word-of-mouth, person-to-person communication. One salesman tells his friends how much he has benefitted. The president of a corporation talks about it to his close friend who is also a business executive. The word gets around!

This report from the *Wall Street Journal* is typical:

> Almost every night after dinner, 26-year-old James Brogger retires to the living room of his home here to listen to a 30-minute recorded lecture. During his lunch hour, Mr. Brogger, who sells label-making machines for Dymo Industries, Inc., Berkeley, Calif., sometimes munches a sandwich in his car so he can pore over some pamphlets.
>
> The records and pamphlets both have the same theme: How to get ahead in business. They are part of a "personal success program" Mr. Brogger bought last January from Success Motivation Institute, Inc., Waco, Texas. Although he's only a quarter of the way through the program Mr. Brogger claims he's gained enough confidence and knowledge to boost his average sales volume by 50%.
>
> The Success Motivation Institute course taken by Mr. Brogger also relies heavily on repetition as a teaching technique. Students listen to one side of a long-playing record for five consecutive days at the same time as they read a script of the record. "This makes the information a part of their life," says Paul J. Meyer, institute president.[1]

Paul Meyer's Basic Principles

What are the basic principles of Paul Meyer's morale-building? He sets them forth simply and clearly:

1. Success is the result of attitude . . . a dedication to personal purpose that refuses to be governed by prevailing conditions or what other people think.

2 Success is the result of habit . . . it depends not so much on doing the unusual, as on doing the commonplace unusually well.

Paul Meyer sometimes calls his type of motivation "attitude motivation." Outcomes are determined largely by motivation. And the best type of motivation is "attitude motivation." [2] He says there are three types of motivation which can be used: "(1) use of threats and fear; (2) financial reward; (3) improvement of work attitudes. This is the strongest of the three and the hardest to accomplish. A man or woman with a *self-motivating attitude* toward his work can be up to 10 times as productive as others."

To complete the picture of Paul Meyer's basic principles, he outlines what he calls "The Million Dollar Personal Success Plan" with five points:

> One: Crystallize Your Thinking . . . determine what specific goal you want to achieve. Then *dedicate* yourself to its attainment with unswerving singleness of purpose, the trenchant zeal of a crusader.

Two: Develop a Plan for Achieving Your Goal, and a Deadline for Its Attainment. Plan your progress carefully: hour-by-hour, day-by-day, month-by-month. Organized activity and maintained enthusiasm are the wellsprings of your power.

Three: Develop a Sincere Desire for the Things You Want in Life. A burning desire is the greatest motivator of every human action. The desire for success implants "success consciousness" which, in turn, creates a vigorous and ever-increasing "habit of success."

Four: Develop Supreme Confidence in Yourself and Your Own Abilities. Enter every activity without giving mental recognition to the possibility of defeat. Concentrate on your *strength,* instead of your weaknesses . . . on your *powers,* instead of your problems.

Five: Develop a Dogged Determination to Follow Through on Your Plan, Regardless of Obstacles, Criticism or Circumstances. Construct your Determination with Sustained Effort—Controlled Attention and Concentrated Energy.

OPPORTUNITIES never come to those who wait . . . they are captured by those who dare to ATTACK.

Repeated Ideas Become Internalized

You have already seen some of the methods of SMI. Cassette recordings are a big part of every course. As you listen to these recordings the ideas become a part of your thinking. As psychologist Dr. J. Clifton Williams, quoted

above, said, "Repetition is the secret." You keep listening
to inspiring ideas and you become inspired. We sometimes
say these ideas become internalized. Some people say that
constantly repeated ideas are finally deposited in the unconscious mind. Whether this is true or not may not be
important. What is important is that ideas of confidence
are repeatedly reinforced until they are literally woven into
your thinking and feeling. Then they begin to show up in
your actions and can finally be developed into productive
habits.

We are reminded here somewhat of the approach of Dr.
Albert Ellis and his method of changing defeatist, negative
patterns of "self-talk" into positive, realistically productive
patterns. We are also reminded of some of the methods of
the New Thought people with their constantly repeated
"affirmations" and "denials."

Cards Are Used, Too

However SMI does not use the denial approach. They
use affirmations only. They feel that the positive is sufficient.
SMI, in one of their courses, has a number of affirmations,
printed on easy-to-use cards. In odd moments the person
may read and repeat these affirmations. This reminds us of a
method used long ago by Dr. Norman Vincent Peale (and a
number of others). He instructed his readers to use cards on
which were printed helpful, faith-building verses of scripture, which they would have available for reading at any

time. Many of Dr. Peale's positive-thinking people would memorize those verses and would repeat them frequently during a day.

With SMI, as with several other systems, you find a technique which emphasizes the importance of patterns of thought. It emphasizes the power of repeated, meaningful language, reviewed frequently to establish patterns of thought, and you can infer from this that they believe that emotion is affected beneficially, although their major emphasis is on action. Certainly much of the motivation to right action is some positive emotion or a combination of positive emotions.

Recordings Will Give You a Daily Boost

The recordings to which you listen are only a part of any given course, but they are an important part. It is interesting to note the subjects of some of these cassette recordings.

One of these is entitled, "As a Man Thinketh" by James Allen. It is taken from an old favorite by the same name which was published in book form many years ago. In the foreword to his book, James Allen stated that his purpose in writing the book was to help the reader understand that ". . . mind is the master-weaver, both of the inner garment of the character, and the outer garment of circumstance, and that, as they may have hitherto woven in ignorance and pain they may now weave in enlightenment and happiness."[3] In the first paragraph of the first chapter he says, "A man is literally *what he thinks. . . .*"

Another of these recordings is one of a very unusual story, "Acres of Diamonds," which in its original form as a lecture was delivered by Dr. Russell H. Conwell more than five thousand times. Each time he delivered it and was paid an honorarium, Dr. Conwell subtracted his expenses and gave the remainder of the honorarium to help some deserving but needy young man pay his college expenses. "Acres of Diamonds" is the true story of an Arab who sold his property to go off on a vain search for diamonds, finally dying in the quest, while the man who bought his property discovered on it one of the richest deposits of diamonds in the world. The point is obvious: that opportunity is here and now and not in some distant place in a remote future.

There are many other recordings, condensing the best ideas for self-fulfillment from more than a score of people whom Paul Meyer calls the Masters of Success of the twentieth century, who give you "the secrets of how to tap your full potential . . . how to transform generalized dreams into specific reality . . . how to materially, spiritually, mentally bring the double crown of success and personal happiness to your life."

These contemporary giants of achievements are typified by Ben Sweetland, expert on human relations and a sales consultant, author of a widely read syndicated newspaper column and of books selling in the millions. There is also Napoleon Hill, whose single volume *Think and Grow Rich* has sold over three million copies. The list includes Alex F. Osborn, the originator of the popular "Brainstorming Technique" and co-founder of a world-famous advertising agency. Another of these masters of success is Elmer Letterman, who has the record of selling over a billion dollars worth of insurance.

These are only a few of the SMI morale builders, the contagion of whose confidence may be delivered to you.

Through listening to inspiring and practical and fascinating recordings, such as Og Mandino's The Greatest Salesman in the World, your attitudes will begin to change and with it your habits, and you are on your way up! With repeated affirmations you will begin to believe in yourself and your ability to hit the bullseye more and more often. But as effective as this is, there is much more.

SMI Helps You Achieve Success in Every Area of Your Life

You have doubtless read enough between the lines already to know that financial success is only a part of what SMI aims at in helping you help yourself. Certainly financial success is a major goal and a realistic one. But the work of SMI goes far beyond this.

Their courses have the objective of helping you achieve optimal satisfactions in every important area of your life.

In one of the courses, called "Your Personal Success Planner," the objective is to help you help yourself develop in six areas of your life: Social, Spiritual, Mental, Physical,

Family, Financial. The course helps you determine exactly what you want in all the important areas of your life.

You write your plan because "a written plan crystallizes thought, and thought motivates action." What you are doing in this course is conditioning yourself to have desirable, positive thought-patterns. The course is a "thought-conditioner" which "will build within you a dedication to purpose that remains undaunted in the face of adversity, that refuses to be governed or controlled by prevailing conditions or what other people think. You will steadily form success-producing attitudes in all the important areas of your life."

Does it actually do what it claims to do? Certainly there are an abundance of voluntary letters of gratitude that demonstrate that it does.

To give an example of this type of testimony, a letter from Honolulu from Lawrence K. Y. Au might serve. Mr. Au wrote, "I can conservatively say that Success Motivation Institute is the main reason for my great success in the insurance business." (He is a representative of Paul Revere Life.) "Moreover, it has made me a better man to my dear wife and three daughters and a more amicable business associate."

This same development of a well-rounded personality as a result of SMI courses is indicated in a portion of a letter from a dentist, Dr. W. A. Russell:

> In the six months since receiving my Personal Success Planner . . . all my relationships have changed! I have learned that attitudes and habits completely control my destiny! It has become a habit for me to

have the attitude of success. I have the habit of crys-
tallizing my thinking, setting specific goals, having
self-confidence and an iron-willed determination to be
successful. One small benefit my wife and I have
received from this new outlook is a doubling of my
personal income in six months.

. . . I have learned to be the architect of my own
business and personal life, that I have within me the
necessary qualities to achieve lasting success . . . the
minute I resolved to develop myself to the fullest, I
became literally, a "New Person."

Most of us have seen so many examples of wealth alone
failing to bring people happiness that we need no convincing
on this point. I can think of numerous dramatic cases. One
person of whom I know made his millions. After this achievement life was completely meaningless for him. He had aimed
at a single goal in life. On reaching it, he found it empty
and unsatisfying. In reaching his single materialistic goal he
had impoverished his mental, cultural, and social development. He was literally a spiritually bankrupt millionaire.
Finally he went into a deep depression and took his own
life. The act of suicide was symbolic of a process that had
been going on internally for many years, for in order to
make his millions, he had already killed the more valuable
parts of his life.

The emphasis of SMI on the development of the whole
personality is a sound one. Suppose you achieve only modest
financial success. Your life can be so enriched in other ways
that you can daily find happiness and satisfaction.

Goals! Goals! Goals!

You will discover another important emphasis with SMI. This has to do with your objectives. In a recent conversation with Curtis B. Matties, vice-president in charge of the production of new courses and programs, he pointed out that one of the weaknesses of many able men was in this area. Men otherwise intelligent, personable, had never clearly defined their goals to themselves. Goal-setting is of supreme importance in achievement.

SMI will help you clarify your long-range goals. But short-range goals are the steps that lead to the long-range goals. The short-range goals must be crystallized. There are also the tangible goals you wish to reach—rewards of a material nature. Other goals are intangible, such as the various facets of personality development, but they are of paramount importance for your happiness.

In achieving these goals, you will find it necessary to know clearly how you now stand in relation to your goals. Are you close to some of them, and a long way off from others?

Another factor in achieving goals is to see clearly what the barriers are that block your way. Only a clear definition of these obstacles will lead you to the next step. How will you overcome these obstacles? Will you break through them or dig under them? Will you go over them or around them?

How will you do this? It can be done, but there must be a plan of attack.

Along with this careful planning of strategy, you are shown how to visualize. Long ago someone said, "Imagination rules the world." Visualization is a conscious sort of imagining. You see the goals achieved. You visualize yourself as having better human relations, as having a better-rounded personality. You see yourself as vital, strong, and healthy. You see yourself prospering in every area of your life. Many of the New Thought teachers also strongly advocate this type of visualization.

You will set definite, realistic target dates for reaching your objectives, and from time to time you will check your progress. You can see that SMI does a clean-sweeping, thorough job of success motivation. They use many of the principles that have been set forth in the earlier chapters of this book.

You Will Benefit From Systematic Self-Analysis

One of those principles which you may have guessed but which has not been spelled out yet in this chapter is the benefit of self-analysis.

Not only does SMI believe as does Dr. Horney that self-analysis is feasible, safe, and practical but they believe that it is imperative if you are to do a real job. Of course, they do not advocate the same method of self-analysis as Dr.

Horney. They teach a down-to-earth, easy to understand, but very systematic and thorough method. Here is the way it goes:

I have spread out before me material which is a part of what is called "Executive Motivation Program." Perhaps the big phrase in this program, as in one mentioned above, is "goal-setting." As a part of this, the first section is devoted to "My Personal Plan of Action." If you were enlisted in this program, this section would also treat the same six areas of your life as mentioned above: Physical, Social, Cultural, Ethical, Financial, and Family Life.

In each of these areas you have a self-evaluation questionnaire. Then you would set up a "priority of values," a putting first things first. Third is a form in which you specifically set up goals. These are both tangible and intangible goals. There are also long- and short-range goals.

First let us examine more specifically the self-evaluation in several areas. In the Physical Development section you will find such questions as these: "Are my attitudes toward my own health in the best long-range interests of my family?" Many times a father is running risks that jeopardize his family's well being. Now he must face this.

Another important question here: "Is my energy level always sufficient for the work I am doing?" If the answer here is no, the reasons could be several—poor diet, such as insufficient protein, or a vitamin deficiency. Or it could be insufficient sleep, or any of a dozen reasons.

Then, "Do I plan adequately for relaxation and exercise?" Also: "Do I have a systematic program of physical fitness?"

And then one that hits many people hard. "Is my weight conducive to optimum health?"

There is a very complete self-evaluation of your physical well-being. After this segment of your self-analysis comes a setting up of a "Priority of Physical Values." What is the most important thing to do about your physical well-being? What is second most important? Third?

Now comes your plan of action for improving your physical well-being. First are the tangible goals you wish to reach in one column and the "obstacles and roadblocks" in a parallel column. There is also a column for the solutions to the problem—how are you going to overcome obstacles? In an other parallel column you note your "Progress to Date," which is feedback or the answer to the question "How am I doing?" There is always a "target date" for every goal. When do you expect to get where you are going?

Suppose your long-range goal was to "lose fifteen pounds." The target date should not be too soon. Crash weight-losing programs are usually dangerous. If you lost only two pounds a week it would take just about seven or eight weeks, and you could do it safely.

In the area of "Social Development" are questions such as, "Am I considerate of others?" and "Am I a good listener?" (Very important!) "Do I have a good sense of humor?" "Do I interrupt people when they are talking?"

Under the heading of Ethical Values you will find, "Do I feel in any moral or ethical way that I am responsible for the welfare of others?" and "Do I have certain religious or moral practices I would retain, even if no one else knew about them?"

Questions under the heading "Financial Development" run like these: "Am I mature in my spending?" "Am I living within my income?" "Is financial development given proper emphasis in my life?" Two subheads under this last question are, "Too much emphasis?" "Too little emphasis?"

These are a few samples from each section of a complete self-evaluation, with emphasis placed on goal-setting, and a plan to achieve every goal.

SMI agrees with others mentioned in previous chapters that self-analysis is profitable and feasible; and SMI gives you a systematic, thorough way of getting the job done!

SMI not only directs you in analyzing yourself but in the use of your time as well. Paul Meyer writes:

> The successful man reflects good health, attractive personality, wealth, social position and the respect of everyone who knows him. But if you search further, delve deeper, you'll discover that there is a single, under-lying factor he shares with every other successful man: he has learned to organize his time. He has organized himself through controlled attention and concentrated energy.
>
> We all know that actually . . . tomorrow never comes. We never do anything or have anything unless we do it and have it NOW. The passage of time can't possibly change failure into success because failure is always failure regardless of the time. Never consider success as a future possibility . . . it exists NOW in YOU . . . and the quickest way to reach it is to organize your time.

He follows this with the following chart:

DAILY TIME USE ANALYSIS

Date

How I Spent My Time	Minutes Wasted and Why
6:00 A.M.	
7:00 A.M.	
8:00 A.M.	
9:00 A.M.	
10:00 A.M.	
11:00 A.M.	
12:00 Noon	
1:00 P.M.	
2:00 P.M.	
3:00 P.M.	
4:00 P.M.	
5:00 P.M.	
6:00 P.M.	
7:00 P.M.	
8:00 P.M.	
9:00 P.M.	
10:00 P.M.	
11:00 P.M.	

Total time wasted

A chart such as the one shown here can be helpful in determining how much productive time you spend each day.

Success Motivation Institute has helpful courses for everyone, from the person who just wants to improve his own personality and increase his satisfactions in life to the small businessman to the most highly trained professionals and the most high-powered executive.

There are numerous courses for salesmen—insurance, intangibles, real estate, mutual funds, retail, automotive, industrial, direct selling, and wholesale route selling. There are courses for executives, for sales managers, and for the independent business owner. The executive secretary is not neglected and neither is the educator. Physicians and lawyers will find courses designed especially for them.

My hat is off, figuratively, to this remarkable group of people at SMI. If you have the business blues, they can show you the way to get rid of them forever.

---

[1] Creedman, Michael. "More Ambitious Men Study How to Succeed in Business by Trying." *The Wall Street Journal,* April 9, 1964.

[2] Meyer, Paul J. "How to Make Your Employees Work as Hard as You Do." *Business Management,* February, 1965.

[3] Allen, James. *As a Man Thinketh.* New York: Thos. Y. Crowell.

CHAPTER 11.

You May Get Help from Experts' Ideas on Mental Health and Religion

OF THE THREE GREAT PIONEERS in promoting mental health, Freud, Adler, and Jung, Freud was the only one who wished to discard religion as a negative value. Freud felt that religion was in the nature of neurotic behavior and that man would be better off without it. However, as you examine the other authorities in the field of mental health, almost without exception, they have agreed that a rational religion is a positive factor in promoting mental health.

You will find that the approach of most of these people is practical. They have in mind what will help the individual live a satisfying, happy, useful life. From this point of view most of them recommend a mature religious faith.

You may find it stimulating to review some of the ideas of these early authorities in the field of mental health.

Adler's Ideas About Religion

In an earlier chapter Alfred Adler was discussed. His emphasis was on a person living a life devoted to the common good, and the personal rewards from following the commandment, "Thou shalt love thy neighbor as thyself." Many would consider this in itself as a very necessary part of vital religion. Adler consistently taught people to live a life of service. This he felt was the antidote to unhappy living. But Adler went far beyond this. We can sum up the essence of Adler's belief in the following quotation:

> 'The best conception hitherto gained for the elevation of humanity is the idea of God. There can be no question that the idea of God really includes within it as a goal the movement towards perfection, and that, as a concrete goal, it best corresponds to the obscure yearnings of human beings to reach perfection. Certainly it seems to me that every one conceives of God in a different way. There are no doubt conceptions of God that fall far short of the principle of perfection; but of its purest form we can say— here—the presentation of the goal of perfection has been successful."

This spiritual conception of Adler's is in complete

contradiction to Freud's materialistic statement that all religion is a form of obsessional neurosis.

Adler's beliefs, like his thoughts, always came from his actual experiences.[1]

Jung's Ideas

If you read the writings of Jung, who by many is considered the most brilliant of these three early psychotherapists, you will find an even fuller expression of the values of religion in mental health.

In his book *Psychology and Religion,* he tells of one of his patients who was suffering from a neurosis.[2] He was an intellectual who prided himself on his scientific viewpoint. Having formerly been a member of a church, he no longer had church affiliations, nor faith in any church as having an intelligent function in a modern world.

Yet Jung's analysis, made over a long period of time, discovered that his patient's emotional difficulties had largely to do with religion. Consequently, Jung's therapy consisted chiefly in bringing his patient to an acceptance of this inner need, not by necessarily returning to his old faith, but by working out a new and vital faith which could be integrated into rational thinking and daily living.

Dr. Jung stated that among all his patients over thirty-five years of age, without exception the central problem was that of finding a "religious outlook on life." [3] These people he said, had fallen ill because they had lost what living religion has to offer, and that none of them was healed without regaining his religious outlook.

Personality Tests and the Religious Life

The testimony of a psychologist, Dr. Henry C. Link, is of especial interest, since he arrived at his conclusions through somewhat objective methods. As a young man in college he had become an agnostic, a position sustained for about twenty years. However, as a psychologist attempting to assist people in solving many personal problems, he found himself more and more frequently using both the concepts and language of religion to communicate psychological ideas to people.

As this process continued, with increasing frequency he fell back on the positive concepts of religion to help people. He discovered that he had adopted again many of the basic beliefs which he had formerly discarded.

For the good of the people whom he counseled, he found himself recommending church attendance, participation in YMCA work, or other similar religious or semi-religious organizations.

Dr. Link came to the conclusion that the findings of psychology were in very close harmony with many of the ideas of religion relating to human emotional and mental well-being. He felt that this conclusion came to him more through the avenues of science than in any other way.[5]

Dr. Link had counseled thousands of people on marital

problems, about employment, loneliness, timidity, human relations in general and a host of other personal difficulties. He served as psychologist with the Adjustment Service of New York City which during two years gave psychological examinations to over 15,000 people. These people were given a total of 73,226 tests. Each person supplied a comprehensive personal history.

One of the findings from this enormous collection of data was that the better balanced and integrated personalities were found among those people who could be classified as religious.[6]

Dr. Link took his own medicine. Finding out that religion was good for others, he felt that it would also be good for him. This constituted his return to religion. He states that a broad spectrum of human problems, ranging from finding a suitable vocation and economic stability, to social and marital happiness, were solved better if people had a truer but more practical set of ideals. This too, he was willing to apply to himself.

The religion Dr. Link writes about is not one of passivity, but of achievement through which the person gains increasing control of his environment rather than becoming its victim. Such a religion makes for personal strength rather than weakness.[7]

*An Authority Discusses the Negative and Positive
Effects of Religion*

When the word "religion" is used, definitions are called for. The word encompasses every type of religion from the most primitive and barbaric to the most advanced altruistic and philosophical systems.

The experts in mental health do not conclude that all religious attitudes, expressions and activities contribute to mental health. This is clearly expressed by Dr. Herbert A. Carroll, formerly professor of psychology at the University of New Hampshire. He states that "religion becomes a negative force when it stresses fear. Fortunately, in our present-day churches, much less is heard about hell than used to be the case. When punishment for sins is stressed the need for emotional security is frustrated." [8]

Yet two pages earlier in the same book, this author stressed a positive religion as contributing to mental health. A religion of faith, he affirms, helps people during the most trying periods of life. It also fills the dependency needs. The person does not feel alone and helpless. He can rely upon a benevolent Diety for help. He adds, "Moreover, worship, including prayer, is a form of catharsis, and catharsis is good for one who is in trouble. Mental hygienists, far from being opposed to religion, welcome the positive contributions religion can make."

A Contemporary Psychiatric Leader Speaks

Concerning the positive approaches to religion, the mental health authorities are very close to making it a unanimous vote in favor. Dr. Karl Menninger, of the world-famous Menninger Clinic, in his latest book *The Vital Balance*, devotes an entire chapter entitled "The Intangibles" to a discussion of faith, hope, and love in the mental and emotional well-being of man.[9] In a previous book he had stated that transference-cures were apt to be temporary since no human can supply all of the love another needs. He continues "it is for this reason that religion in its positive faith-and-love aspects furnishes such people an incalculable, immeasurable therapeutic benefit. It is doubtless true that religion has been the world's greatest psychiatrist through the centuries." [10]

From The Textbooks on Psychotherapy

In one of the most widely used and comprehensive textbooks on psychotherapy, the author, Dr. Lewis R. Wolberg, Clinical Professor of Psychiatry at New York Medical College, repeatedly refers to the therapeutic benefits deriving from a positive religious faith.[11] In one place he sums this up by saying, "The goal of psychotherapy is not too different from that of a constructive religion. The latter, an affirmation of man's faith which is a basic requirement for human existence, like psychotherapy encourages self-actualizing tendencies. Psychotherapy and religion are thus mutually compatible rather than antagonistic. . . ."

Few psychiatrists have been franker in acknowledging the therapeutic value of religion than William A. Sadler, chief psychiatrist and director of the Chicago Institute of Research and Diagnosis. He devotes an entire chapter in his volume *The Practice of Psychiatry* to the subject.[12] At the beginning of the chapter he writes, "Worship renews the spirit as sleep renews the body."

He has much to say on therapy through prayer. He suggests that prayer is one of the best ways of catharsis for repressed resentments and fears; that confession in prayer is catharsis for guilt, that positive prayer is an exercise which tends to integrate the personality. He writes, "When we set ourselves to this work of collecting or re-collecting the scattered pieces of ourselves, we begin a task which, if carried to its natural conclusions, ultimately becomes prayer."

He recounts the case of a woman patient for whom the prognosis was none too good. Dr. Sadler, in view of her symptoms and history, felt that it would be more than a year before she would show signs of improvement. He was amazed to find that in one week's time the patient had improved more than he had expected in a year. She had been under treatment by Dr. Lena Sadler, William Sadler's wife.

When he asked the patient how the change had been effected, the woman answered, "Dr. Lena taught me how to pray."

The Importance of Belief

The late Dr. Gordon Allport of Harvard makes the statement that the fact is that "what a man believes to a large extent determines his mental and physical health . . . Religious belief . . . often turns out to be the most important belief of all." [13] He tells about one psychiatrist who, although a skeptic himself, when he discovers a patient is religious, recognizes that in the long run his religion will be the strongest factor in bringing about a cure. Still another psychiatrist on a purely practical basis directs his patients in helping other patients because the psychiatrist knows that love is the greatest of all therapeutic agents both to the one loving and the one being loved.

The attitude and the behavior of love, as expressed in religion, build mental and emotional health. So does the attitude and behavior of faith. Religion may point the way to creativity and self-realization. Religious confession relieves the burden of guilt and brings an inner emotional cleansing. From religious faith life achieves its highest meaning. And through the deep currents of genuine religious experience, the person may come into his own in self-realization and creative living. For these reasons the experts in mental health advocate constructive religious faith as a major factor in promoting the total well-being of man.

---

[1] Bottome, Phyllis. *Alfred Adler.* New York: The Vanguard Press, 1957, p. 56.

[2] Jung, Carl G. *Psychology and Religion.* New Haven, Conn.: Yale University Press, 1938.

[3] Jung, Carl G. *Modern Man in Search of a Soul.* New York: Harcourt, Brace, 1933, p. 264.

[4] Link, Henry C. *The Return to Religion.* New York: The Macmillan Co., 1936, p. 5.

[5] *Ibid.,* p. 7.

[6] *Ibid.,* p. 13.

[7] *Ibid.,* pp. 15-16.

[8] Carroll, Herbert A. *Mental Hygiene,* 4th ed. Englewood Cliffs, New Jersey: Prentice-Hall, 1964, p. 280.

[9] Menninger, Karl. *The Vital Balance.* New York: The Viking Press, 1964, pp. 357-400.

[10] _____. *Man Against Himself.* New York: Harcourt, Brace, 1938.

[11] Wolberg, Lewis R. *The Technique of Psychotherapy.* New York: Grune and Stratton, 1967, pp. 231-232.

[12] Sadler, Wm. S. *The Theory and Practice of Psychiatry.* St. Louis, Mo.: The C. V. Mosby Co., 1936.

[13] Allport, Gordon. *The Individual and His Religion.* New York: The Macmillan Co., 1951, p. 79.

CHAPTER 12.

You Can Unlearn the Emotions You Have Learned

Are You Born with a Certain Temperament?

ONE OF THE REASONS why people are sometimes pessimistic is because they feel they were born a certain way and that nothing can be done about it. Many parents have this attitude about their children, and the attitude is contagious. The children catch it!

The parents say, "Joey was born with a bad temper. Charlie was born with a bright and happy disposition." So Joey grows up feeling there is nothing he can do about his ugly temper. Charlie grows up confident that he will always be cheery because he was born that way.

It is true that we are born with certain characteristics

140

that can't be changed. The color of our eyes, our finger-prints, hair color and a long list of physical characteristics are among these traits.

It is also true that children are born with different temperaments. This may be due to a number of factors. For example, the size and activity of certain glands may influence temperament. Other physical traits may also have an influence.

Your Temperament Can Be Changed

But because you were born with a certain glandular structure does not mean that you cannot control your behavior and your emotional states.

The pioneer psychologist who gave some dramatic and convincing demonstrations of the learning of emotional reactions was John B. Watson at Johns Hopkins University. This account may be found in almost any elementary psychology text.[1]

Dr. Watson experimented with a young boy named Albert in a medical clinic. First a white rat was turned loose in the room where Albert was crawling around. Albert was curious about the rat, went over to it and stretched out his hand to touch it. Before he did, the psychologist struck two metal bars together making a loud disagreeable noise. This was the beginning of a conditioning process. Each time Albert approached the rat the unpleasant noise occurred.

Albert's association with the rat for this reason became unpleasant. Finally Albert would begin to whimper when the rat was brought into the room. Originally attracted to the rat, Albert had learned to fear the rat and to avoid it.

Dr. Mary Cover Jones, one of Watson's former students, demonstrated the reverse of Watson's experiment.[2] She, too, had access to a clinic in which there were children who had a pet rabbit with which they played often.

One little fellow by the name of Peter was deathly afraid of the rabbit, apparently having somewhere learned to fear a small animal. Now the question was could Peter unlearn his fear? Dr. Jones began a slow conditioning process to determine if this could be accomplished.

While Peter was eating, the rabbit would be brought into the room some distance away. Now a pleasant activity was associated with a feared animal. Gradually, over a number of days, the rabbit was brought closer and closer to Peter as he ate. Another tactic was to let Peter watch the other children as they happily played with the rabbit.

Little by little, Peter lost his fear of the rabbit. Finally he allowed the rabbit to be brought quite close to where he was eating. The great triumph arrived when Peter at last took the rabbit in his arms. His fear had been conquered by the learning process. It had been unlearned.

Yes, physiologically and temperamentally we are born different from each other. But learning can make the difference. We human beings are of all living creatures most fortunate. We have an almost unlimited capacity for learning. We can teach one another. We can teach ourselves. We can learn to adapt to all sorts of varying conditions. Most of that adaptability is through the learning process.

It may be true that Joey was born with a temper that was harder to control than Charlie's. But Joey can learn to control his temper. He can learn to direct his aggression in such a way that it will not hurt him and others. He can channel the energy generated by his aggression into bettering his environment, conquering the elements, exploring his world, achieving vast success in business.

Your moods have been learned somewhere in the past, perhaps from a parent, another child or a relative. If the mood is a positive one, well and good. If it is a negative one, you can change it to a positive one.

"Ruth is a born pessimist!" exclaimed her mother. Ruth may have been born with a temperament inclined toward pessimism. It is more likely that Ruth learned to be pessimistic because of her mother's pessimism, or that of an aunt or a grandmother. Even so Ruth can learn not to be pessimistic. She can learn to substitute optimism for pessimism. She can cultivate the habit, the daily, the hourly, persistent habit of confidence toward herself and her world. Ruth can change herself. Ruth can better her attitudes. Ruth is human, and the best learners in our world are human beings.

All Sorts of Changes in Behavior are Possible

Since the time of John B. Watson, experiments in human conditioning have been so numerous that they would fill

volumes. Dr. H. J. Eysenck, an English psychologist who is
an authority on human conditioning, gives a long list of
deep-seated personality disturbances which have been successfully treated with conditioning processes, among them
obsessional neurosis, alcoholism, bronchial asthma, and hys-
terical aphonia.[3]

Again at Johns Hopkins, Dr. K. S. Lashley conditioned
reflexive behavior, measuring human salivation at the sight,
the feel, or the smell of a candy bar.[4]

Even the behavior of animals, some of which has for
centuries been thought to be instinctive, lends itself to considerable alteration. Psychologist Z. Y. Kuo performed a
series of carefully controlled experiments with cats, rats, and
mice in a variety of relationships.[5] He raised kittens with
rats as cagemates. Even when the kitten reached maturity,
the cat would never attack the rat. Out of eighteen cases,
only three cats raised in the same cages with rats killed rats
at all and these were a dissimilar type of rat from the cagemate. Mr. Kuo writes, "And if one insists that the cat has an
instinct to kill a rat, I must add that it has an instinct to
love the rat, too."

If a kitten grew up in the same cage as a rat, it was not
only tolerant of rats, but became attached to its cagemate.
Not even seeing other cats kill and eat rats changed its attitude of tolerance and attachment.[6] If the rat was taken out
of the cage, the cat became restless and was not at ease until
the rat was returned to the cage. As stated above, these
experiments demonstrated that there was no unalterable
predetermined behavior pattern of cats toward rats and

mice. The entire pattern of circumstances in which these relationships took place was the deciding factor in determining the nature of the relationships, which ran the gamut from the usual rat-killing cat to the cat which would neither kill nor eat a rat even under conditions of extreme food deprivation and after seeing other cats kill and eat rats. There may be an "instinctive" basis for cats killing rats and mice. If so, it becomes evident that the instinctive pattern can be altered.

Anger, Fear, and Depression Can Be Changed

It is common knowledge that inherent in the nature of man are certain mechanisms underlying anger reactions. One of the keys in this mechanism is the adrenal medulla with its hormones of adrenaline and noradrenaline. Evidence also points to the hypothalamus as a control center influencing the mechanism. There is little question that in both man and the infrahuman animals, anger reactions generally are innate and have a survival value under certain conditions. So much then for the inherent mechanism that results in anger reactions. An animal under threat, particularly if it is a continued threat, or an animal that feels trapped or cornered, may attack and survive as a result of an inherent survival mechanism.

Your basic emotional responses have a survival value, too. Under extreme emotion many times man's energy may be so mobilized that he seems to have almost superhuman strength and endurance. But in today's world, many of the fear-and-anger responses of people have no survival value at all. People through conditioning processes become habitually fearful or hostile when there is no real reason for either emotion. The organism is constantly overmobilized and under needless harmful stress. Now the value of these emotions is negative. They have become a threat to survival rather than a force for survival. As such they should be altered.

With excessive fear, depression may result. The person is constantly fearful that he is going to make a mistake. He constantly dreads and expects failure. Is it any wonder that he has the blues?

Or he becomes needlessly hostile to people around him. Because of poor human relations he is repeatedly rebuffed and frustrated. Again, is it any wonder that he grows depressed?

Fortunately, the habitual fear and hostility can be changed. Man can change himself. He can replace fear with faith, anger with good will. His relations with other people and his world in general now are running smoothly, lubricated with trust and friendship.

You can improve your emotional habits and, by so doing, improve your health and your prospects. Many methods for doing this have been suggested in the chapters above. Others will be described in the chapters to follow. From these you will be able to find those methods that work for you. Applying these methods, you ought to be able to maintain yourself on a habitual level of high morale.

You should be able to create the conditions under which pessimism will disappear and intelligent optimism will reign in its place.

Your life should become a series of experiences that will increase your faith and never weaken it. This faith will be in yourself and your ability to reach your goals. It will be a growing faith in the positive traits of others. As you have this attitude, more and more people will exercise only those positive traits when dealing with you.

You can establish a growing faith in the ultimate good in the universe. Such a faith will actually build for you a good universe, just as the opposite view could result in a bad universe. We can make ourselves pretty much what we will. We can make our environment a happy one. We can create our own high destiny.

---

[1] Watson, John B. *Psychology from the Standpoint of a Behaviorist.* Philadelphia: J. B. Lippincott, 1919, pp. 202-206.

[2] Jones, Mary C. "A laboratory study of fear: the case of Peter," *The Pedogogical Seminary* (1924): 31, 308-315.

[3] Eysenck, H. J. *Experiments in Personality,* vols. I and II. London: Routledge, 1960.

[4] Watson, John B. *Op. cit.,* pp. 30-31.

[5] Kuo, Z. Y. "The genesis of the cat's response to the rat," *Journal of Comparative Psychology,* Vol. II, 1930, pp. 30-35.

[6] _____, "Further study on the behavior of the cat towards the rat," *Journal of Comparative Psychology,* Vol. 25, 1933, pp. 1-8.

CHAPTER 13.

You Can Recondition Yourself

HAPPINESS IS AN EMOTIONAL REACTION. Sadness is also an emotion or combination of emotions. Because of our emotions we are depressed or elated or somewhere in between. If we are depressed, life does not seem satisfying, our achievement is usually poor, and our relations with others far from rewarding.

Sadness apparently is in large part learned. It can be unlearned, or in the language of the early behaviorists, "unconditioned." Happiness can be learned. In fact, sadness is unlearned by replacing it with happiness.

A Brief Review Might be Helpful

The methods of combatting depression that have been discussed in preceding chapters all have to do with the un-learning of the attitude of sadness. and the learning of its opposite, an attitude of optimism and joy. It might be a profitable exercise here to review some of these suggestions and see how they fit into the idea of unlearning certain mental-emotional attitudes and learning others.

The part of Dr. Alfred Adler's approach that was empha-sized was the idea of getting away from egocentricity or self-centeredness by beginning to serve others. In the first place, just doing something positive is preferable to wallow-ing in self-pity and pessimism. In serving others, you have a feeling of being valuable and that is a happy feeling. Others also respond to us favorably when we make our contribution of service. This in turn sets up emotions of pleasure. By directing our thoughts away from ourselves toward others, we are substituting feelings of pleasure for feelings of dis-pleasure. As this process becomes habitual, an attitude of optimism becomes habitual.

Next, by learning habits of progressive relaxation, we substitute a beneficial muscular habit for a negative habit. The negative habit was one of needless muscular tensions that accompany the negative emotions of fear, anger, and depression.

The undesirable emotions and the muscular tensions

have developed together. By breaking the muscular tensions, the strength of the harmful emotions is weakened. Also, by using this practice, we are getting our minds off our unhappiness and directing our thinking toward a positive and pleasure-producing relaxation activity.

The talking-it-out procedure is a matter of bringing our troubles out into the open where they are less threatening than if we tuck them away in the hidden recesses of the mind. Simply by sharing them with another person they also become less threatening. This method has sometimes been called a method of desensitization.

The "writing-it-out-of-your-system" and the self-analysis plans help because, by both methods, the causes of difficulties become clearer and more easily dealt with. When we learn the causes, we can also learn to eliminate the causes. We then initiate more satisfying behavior.

Both Dr. Ellis' rational therapy and substituting positive "self-talk" for negative, and the approach of the various religions advocating positive instead of negative thinking, are really methods of unconditioning and reconditioning.

Success Motivation Institute combines a number of these approaches—such as self-analysis, the power of positive thinking, and working definitely toward clear-cut positive goals. The SMI inspirational records set up processes of positive thinking and feeling in place of the negative ones.

There are three psychotherapists of note who also have systems of unlearning the negative by learning the positive which might be worth studying.

A Common-Sense Approach to Personal Problems

One is Dr. E. Lakin Phillips, a psychologist who practices what he calls "assertion-structured therapy." [1] Dr. Phillips says that our lives are guided by assertions we make about ourselves and also about our relationships with others. These assertions are the hypotheses by which we live. Every day our conduct is determined greatly by these assumptions.

These assumptions, he says, are either confirmed or disconfirmed. If the assumption does not work out it is disconfirmed, in which case there would be disappointment. The truly unhappy person is the one who habitually lives by assumptions that are being disconfirmed.

This person does not learn from his mistakes. He keeps repeating them over and over. As a result, he is an unhappy person.

Improvement would come about through the person beginning to understand what assumptions he was making that were constantly disconfirmed and making him unhappy. As he sees these assumptions, he can substitute for them assumptions that will be confirmed. This will give him satisfaction. Here is an example.

An idealistic young woman married and wanted children. She became pregnant and was convinced that she was going to have a sweet little girl, upon whom she could lavish her affection. She dreamed of how she was going to dress her child in dainty feminine clothing, all harmonious in color and perfect in design. So, against the advice of her doctor and her husband, she began to prepare for a girl.

As you have anticipated, she had a boy. He was an active, rambunctious little fellow. For a long time the mother was unhappy about the situation. She began to expect too much of her son and was usually disappointed. Cleanliness and neatness made no particular sense to him as he learned to crawl, walk, and play.

His mother would bathe him, dress him in clean, beautiful clothing, only to have him turn up filthy in half an hour. Fortunately, this young mother, partly through her doctor, partly through her husband (who was overjoyed at having a rowdy son), saw how unrealistic her expectations had been. She adjusted to the situation as it really was rather than her fantasy. Otherwise she and her family would have been most unhappy.

In a similar case I observed that the mother was completely unrealistic and insisted upon dressing and treating her boy like a girl. Consequently, there was great unhappiness for many people.

I know a young man who boasted that he took pride in taking unethical shortcuts to reach his goals. Not long ago he suffered a serious setback because of this attitude. This would not have happened if his assumption had been that he would reach his goal, using ethical means, and giving the best he had in return for the reward he expected.

What hypotheses do we live by? What are our expectations? Do we learn from our mistakes? If we are unhappy, what are the disconfirmations that make us so?

Marriage is sometimes an unhappy affair because either husband or wife is expecting of the marital partner a pattern of behavior that is completely unrealistic. You have probably known wives who tried to make their husbands over to fit some sort of dream of the faultless male. Or you have known husbands who expected their wives to be scintilating socially, perfect cooks and housekeepers, and faultless mothers.

The assertion-structured approach is basically a common-sense approach. It involves enough self-analysis to point out why you are unhappy. Then it suggests selecting goals that are reachable and at the same time will bring real rewards of personal satisfaction. Many personal problems could be solved and life could be made happier if you followed this recipe.

If Overinhibition Is Your Trouble

Many people are overinhibited. Some are too uninhibited. Either extreme makes for unhappy living. For a few minutes, let us think about an overdose of inhibition.

The person who has this is too self-critical. He watches his every move, his every impulse. He is overly cautious. He rarely ever turns loose. He is too introspective. He may experience excessive guilt, and sometimes over trivial things.

As far as experiencing and showing spontaneous emotion is concerned, this is foreign to his behavior. Spontaneous laughter is rare. A genuine show of affection and warmth is equally rare. His life is impoverished because of the over-control of his emotions.

Psychologist Andrew Salter has much to say about this process of overinhibition. He feels that most neurotic behavior is traceable to something of this sort. He says that "the diagnosis is always inhibition." [2]

Whether he is right about this is not the question here. Dr. Salter had dealt with many cases of people who were too inhibited. He might even be called a specialist in this line. He helps people break through the barriers of overinhibition. He has a formula for this. Some of this formula I am skeptical about. I give it here because it has its amusing aspects and because, even if it may be overstated, Dr. Salter has an approach that is well worth considering.[3] There are six points in his formula.

First, engage in "feeling-talk." Express your spontaneous emotions in speech. "I feel wonderful today!" or "Monday morning gives me a pain-in-the-neck!" Out with it, whatever you feel, good or bad! Put it into words that express your emotions.

Second, let your face show how you feel. If you feel great wear a broad smile. If you are angry, scowl. If you are afraid, let your face screw up with fear.

Now we come to some points where many people begin to question the validity of Salter's formula, because his third point is "contradict and attack." If you disagree, say so. If you dislike what is being said, tell it in no uncertain terms. Dr. Salter says that this is just giving emotional content to the facts.

Have you ever been with a person who was so sweetly agreeable that you quickly tired of his company? Sometimes life is made much more interesting if a person questions your point of view and advances ideas and opinions that are different from yours. So I would not completely reject this point. Still I am not going around looking for a fight, either, and if my attitude toward others is always "contradict and attack," this is exactly what might happen.

The fourth point is to use the pronoun "I" deliberately and as much as possible in your conversation. This, too, according to my opinion, could be easily overdone. Yet what we like to hear is the personal. The overinhibited person needs to bring more of the personal into his conversation.

The fifth point is always good for a laugh when you read it or talk about it. When you are praised or complimented, "agree with it." If someone says, "You certainly made a good speech," Dr. Salter instructs the one praised to respond with something like this, "Yes, I was in good form, wasn't I?" But he also instructs that you try to find something nice to say to your complimenter, *if you can!* Again, maybe we have too much false modesty. If you think you made a good speech, why deny it?

My opinion of what should be done in this case would be to thank the person warmly and to tell him that you are glad he enjoyed it.

The last point is "improvise!" Live for right now. Get the most out of life now! In an argument, express your opinion whether you have the facts to back it up or not. "Live now," he writes, "and tomorrow will take care of itself." You will recognize this was said beautifully more than nineteen hundred years ago.

Some of Dr. Salter's recipe may sound like how to lose friends and infuriate people. But if you are overinhibited, he has a message for you.

Loosen up! Be more spontaneous. Let your feelings out with words, gestures, and facial expressions. You are a feeling person, live like one. Don't be a monotonous conformist. You have ideas. Express them. Put the most into today, the right now. Live every moment to the fullest.

If you do this you will be a more interesting person. You will get more out of life and put more into it. You will have more friends that really care about you. So I would say, to the overinhibited, take a dose of Salter (no pun intended) and see how it works.

Inhibition of a Certain Kind Can Be Therapeutic

Dr. Joseph Wolpe, psychiatrist, has evolved a system of therapy from which any person may get tips for self-improvement. Dr. Wolpe calls his system "psychotherapy by reciprocal inhibition."

Theoretically it follows rather sound procedures, and Dr. Wolpe claims 90 per cent efficiency in improving neurotic conditions.

The principle of this method of personality betterment is that if a person can set up a positive response in a stimulus situation which originally called forth negative and disturbing responses, his disturbances can be overcome.

Let us take an imaginary example. Suppose a person has a fear response to dogs. If he can set up a situation in which his response will be pleasant to dogs, the old response will be inhibited and can be lost. This is exactly the same principle that Dr. Mary Cover Jones used in curing Peter of his fear of the rabbit.

She attempted to set up pleasant responses to inhibit the old fear response, and in order to do it she had the rabbit brought into the room where Peter was eating, and also had other children play with the rabbit in Peter's presence. Finally, fear of the rabbit was inhibited by the new pleasure responses toward the rabbit.

Of course, Dr. Wolpe's method involves much more than this simple procedure, but the principle is the same. You might be interested to know his system.

He has his patient make out a list of situations that cause anxiety, starting with the worst at the top and the weakest at the bottom.

Usually he then trains the person to relax systematically. Next, under hypnosis the subject is caused to relax as much as possible and to imagine himself in the weakest anxiety-creating situation.

Since relaxation is antagonistic to anxiety, the subject will feel no anxiety. Then he is moved up to a more severe anxiety situation. This goes on until the greatest anxiety situation is countered with relaxation.

Now the subject is instructed to react to the real-life situations with relaxation. This presumably inhibits the anxiety.

In an earlier chapter in which we discussed Jacobson's Progressive Relation, we also talked about a group of psychiatrists who were using this procedure with their patients quite successfully.

Dr. Wolpe, on occasion, will also have the subject use positive assertions to counter negative feelings. This sort of thing we found with both Dr. Albert Ellis and all the positive thinkers, who use positive assertions to conquer negative feelings and overcome negative behavior.

I know a graduate student who used this basic principle quite successfully in a practical way. He found much of the study required of him tedious and depressing. How could he overcome these negative feelings which would defeat him in mastering these boring but necessary intellectual tasks?

He began inviting other graduate students to study with him, making it a truly social affair with refreshments. In such a way, a depressing task became a very pleasant one, and the tedious study much more acceptable.

Suppose you find yourself depressed on Monday mornings. What pleasurable activities could you initiate that would combat these feelings of depression? Perhaps you could have a special treat for breakfast or wear clothing that is particularly becoming and pleasing.

You may remember that the Success Motivation Institute furnishes morale-building recordings to be played as one prepares to go to work. I know one person who plays his favorite stereo-records if he feels blue in the morning as he gets up. He hums along with the records and soon forgets the blues.

Each person is different. Each situation is different. But with searching and ingenuity, I have every confidence that you can find the morale-building stimuli for yourself that will inhibit the blues by setting up a chain reaction of pleasant emotions within you.

---

[1] Phillips, E. Lakin. *Psychotherapy, a Modern Theory and Practice.* Englewood Cliffs, N. J.: Prentice-Hall, 1956.

[2] Salter, Andrew. *Conditioned Reflex Therapy.* New York: Creative Age Press, 1949, p. 104.

[3] *Ibid.*, pp. 97-103.

CHAPTER 14.

You Can Read Those Blues Away

You Can Read for Fun and for Profit

THAT YOU ARE READING THIS BOOK indicates the one obvious fact that you do a certain amount of reading for self-improvement. You will not be disappointed. You can improve yourself in many ways through reading.

Much of this chapter will be quite personal. There is a scarcity of reliable studies investigating the effects of reading on personality. So we have to rely on observation, reports, and, to a certain extent, on opinion.

I grew up in a reading family. Everybody read. We learned to read early and we have kept on reading. I remember one incident that happened when I was three years old.

Our large family were all in the living room, except my baby brother who was asleep. Everybody, including my five-and-a-half-year-old brother was reading. I was not to be outdone. I got a magazine—no pictures in it to give me a clue—and held it as if I, too, were reading.

My father smiled and said to me, "Frank, you're reading upside down." He straightened out the magazine for me. Then everybody went on reading.

Very early all of us had many periods of happiness from reading. There were family books that my father or mother read aloud to all of us. Then the older children read to the younger. And by the time most of us were five years old, we began reading for ourselves.

I can recall many hours of sheer pleasure as I lay on the floor flat on my stomach in the company of a fascinating book. Today the same holds true for the joy I get out of reading.

Positive Reading Can Displace Negative Feeling

Books can bring you happiness in many ways and in so doing can banish feelings of gloom. If you are in a period of depression, a book may distract you, get your mind off yourself and your troubles, and at least temporarily offset your low feelings. I know one person who has adopted this as a regular strategy. He keeps an interesting book handy, and if he finds himself becoming the victim of any negative emotions, he begins reading his book. He finds this a wonderful antidote.

I know a man who was stricken with a serious illness that left him pessimistic about his future. In his hospital room he had with him a book by Nevil Shute, *The Trustee of the Tool Room*. This is a wholesome book, full of subtle humor and human interest. The man and his wife took turns reading the book aloud, pausing frequently for laughter. This was real fun for them and had a great deal to do with counteracting the pessimism engendered by the illness.

It is hard for one person to tell another just which books will be the medicine his mind and emotions need. Tastes differ widely. Needs also vary a great deal. So reading for self-improvement is a most individual affair. Many people liked *The Trustee of the Tool Room*. At least many of my friends reported on it favorably. But you might not find it your book at all. I have found all of Nevil Shute's books worth reading, but this is a highly personal reaction.

The Wrong Kinds of Books May Increase Negative Feelings

Is there a negative side of the picture? Are there books you can read that leave you more depressed than you were to begin with? Are there books that would leave you angry or fearful? You know the answer. But what books will do this to you? This you must discover for yourself.

Many so-called escape books depend almost entirely upon suspense. Suspense is largely a fear reaction and it may have quite a lot of anger in it, too. You become identified with some character in the book. This character is put under threat and so you are vicariously also under threat. In many books the suspense is built up skillfully chapter by chapter until your system is so full of adrenalin and noradrenaline that you could drain it off into bottles and compete with the wholesale drug companies. Do you think this is good for you?

We have some quite reliable evidence about viewing television and movies. Dr. Albert Bandura at Stanford has exposed children to TV violence.[1] He has discovered that TV violence caused children to engage in very aggressive behavior and also that the TV violence has something to do with the direction the children's violence will take. A Canadian investigator, Dr. Walters of the University of Toronto, discovered about the same sorts of reactions in adults after watching TV violence.[2]

What About Suspense Fiction?

In some of the escape literature, you escape into fear or anger, or both. Is this good for you or bad for you?

The answer is not clear. Some people get release from their suppressed anger through reading books about aggression. Others apparently do not. Some readers get release from their own inner fears as they live through fear experiences in literature. Other readers only grow more fearful. We need more scientific evidence on this point, but as it now stands each person must find out what benefits him.

Many of the experts say that we are all overstimulated today through movies, TV, radio, and reading. They say this is true not only in regard to fear and anger reactions but in regard to sex. With all this overstimulation of the emotions, our behavior begins to be affected.

Fiction That Depends Upon Characterization

There is fiction of a different kind, not depending upon mere suspense but written in such a way that we become chiefly interested in the characters of the book. There is fiction that is filled with beauty of thought and language. An example of this is James Norman Hall's *The Far Lands*. Here is escape into a world of wonder and goodness. Another similar book that stands out in my memory is Ray Bradbury's *The Martian Chronicles*.

Unfortunately, books like these and like those of Neville Shute are all too rare. Some of this type of fiction may not be classified as great literature, but the question I am considering here is what will build you up personally. What kinds of fiction are emotionally healthy for the reader?

I have in the last two years gone to two plays that were rated tops by the critics. They were well-acted. But in each case I felt as I left that I had been wallowing in muck. If I can help it, I won't do that to myself!

The fiction of Lloyd C. Douglas has hardly been classified as great literature. And while it has been several years since I read his books, when I finished one, I always felt more hopeful and confident about myself and my fellow-beings. I always wanted to be better and do better. So I have eliminated myself from joining the ranks of the high-brows and the literati, and I could not be less bothered.

You Can Escape too Much

Escape of this kind should only be for short periods. Each of us has his own work to do and reality to cope with. A woman of my acquaintance literally buried herself in fiction. She read constantly. She borrowed books by the dozen and read them all. She lived in a never-never land of fictional characters. She escaped all the time. She evaded life. This is a prime example of an activity which is healthful in moderation, but which in excess becomes harmful.

Positive Reading for Information

Reading for information, while quite different from the so-called escape fiction, may help to eliminate or reduce negative emotion. I have a friend who is constantly enlarging his knowledge about his profession. This is positive thinking, too, and displaces the negative emotions of sadness, fear, or anger. He is a man who stands high in his business and is gaining ground every day.

There are many books one can read for self-understanding. This would help in self-analysis. There are psychology books that are written for popular consumption. There are also similar books on philosophy. There are books on social psychology and on sociology which deal with bettering human relations.

Many books written by competent authors aim at building morale. The public libraries nearly all have long lists of such books. One author of a widely read self-help book testified that reading such books literally transformed his life.

There are many of these morale-building books that will not fill your needs. But there are a surprising number of soundly conceived, well-written books, that contribute to self-understanding and build morale at the same time.

Dip Into a Book Enough to See If It Will Do Anything for You

I started a book last night that came highly recommended. It is a big seller and has had some complimentary reviews in the right places.

But I found it full of sordid characters and sordid events. I know there are people like this in the world; I have come in contact with a few. But I don't spend any time in their company. Why, then, should I spend the time with the people in this book?

Fortunately, I do not have to. So I laid the book aside

after reading enough of it to know it was not going to add anything to me at all. I would rather spend the equivalent time looking at the stars or at flowers or birds or listening to sublime music on the stereo.

Why waste time on a book that might leave me feeling worse than when I started? I highly recommend dipping into a book enough to find out if it will do something positive for you. If not, throw it aside as quickly as you would a piece of meat that is spoiled. Why contaminate yourself when you can spend the same amount of time adding to your store of inner treasures?

---

[1] Bandura, Albert. "What TV Violence Can Do to a Child." *Look*, Oct. 22, 1963, pp. 46-52.

[2] *Ibid.*, p. 52.

CHAPTER 15.

Your Body Can Help You Beat the Blues

WHAT HAPPENS TO YOUR BODY when you are depressed? Are there physical strategies that can help you overcome low morale? The answer to the second question is yes, and most of this chapter is devoted to how. For the answer to the first question, we must look to research.

Scientific Research on the Physiology of Depression

Some of this research has already been mentioned in Chapter 2, where you read about Progressive Relaxation. Dr. Edmund Jacobson found that sometimes people who

168

were depressed had excessive muscular tensions. Since Dr. Jacobson's research this finding has been further verified.

Nearly always anxiety precedes or accompanies depression. Using the electromyogram, which indicates muscular tensions, it was found that with anxiety, neck muscles were tense. Using a tremorgram it was established that, during anxiety, there was a marked increase of trembling in the fingers.[1] Pulse rate, blood pressure, and respiration were also affected.

When the anxiety was accompanied with hostility, arm muscles showed tension; and when the anxiety involved sex guilt, leg-muscles showed tension.

Another type of physical reaction has been observed in laboratory studies of depression. Physiological processes are retarded.[2] Movements are slower, speech is slower, blood pressure is low, heart and lung action are slow, digestive processes are below par.

Two medical investigators had an unusual case and one which shed considerable light on digestive processes during emotions.[3] They observed a patient whose esophagus had been severely burned and in which scar tissue had closed the opening. In order for the patient to be fed the stomach had to be opened surgically, following which its processes could be observed. Under conditions of either sadness or fear the mucous membrane would turn pale. The contractions of the alimentary canal, necessary in the digestive process, were also retarded as part of the reaction pattern.

Our common experiences are in harmony with the scientific evidence. When you have the blues, you are usually slower, duller, more sluggish. As we have noticed before, the condition of the body may affect our emotional states and vice versa. There is interaction between physical well-being and mental-emotional well-being. Improving one helps to improve the other.

It appears that we could get rather general agreement from the authorities in the field that increasing your general physical well-being will usually positively affect your morale.

Exercise May Help You Beat the Blues

In the last few years we have seen a revival of interest in exercise. One of the reasons for this was the large percentage of men whose draft boards discovered that they are physically weak and unfit.

Another reason has been the relationships between exercise and heart disease and other diseases of the circulatory system. Those who exercise regularly and sufficiently with the right activity apparently are not as subject to coronary and vascular diseases as those who don't.

There are reasons enough for exercise to be considered as a morale builder. If you know the probability of your becoming the victim of some such disorder is greatly lessened by regular, sufficient exercise, your spirits should be considerably lifted.

The benefits go further. As your circulation is improved, the general functioning of your body improves, and other things being equal, there should be improved digestion, skin condition, muscle-tone, better sleeping habits, and perhaps a long list of other improvements. This is not to say that exercise is going to usher in a millenium. It is one of several factors having to do with well-being of the physical organism.

A recent, readable and popular paperback book, based upon objective studies, is *Aerobics*, written by Dr. Kenneth H. Cooper of the U.S. Air Force.[4] He had large numbers of subjects to work with, of all sizes, ages, and physical conditions, both males and females.

The oxygenation of the blood through exercise is one of Dr. Cooper's emphases, for oxygen well-supplied to all parts of the body is one of the essentials for good health. The brain needs a great deal of exygen to function adequately. Through stimulated circulation and breathing, says Dr. Cooper, the body may be adequately supplied with oxygen.

As you exercise, the size of the blood vessels increases. Not only that, but new blood vessels actually come into being through exercise. Probably he is referring to new capillaries.

Dr. Cooper states that not only does exercise help a person physically, but brings about betterment both emotionally and mentally. He says that all the studies done on the subject find a positive correlation between being in good physical condition and mental alertness.[5] This correlation extends to emotional stability as well. Dr. Cooper cites a study made of a group of men who were middle-aged executives, earning high salaries, who prior to beginning the program were inactive and one-third of them coronary types. Tests showed these men to be depressed and defensive prior to beginning the program. Depression disappeared after these men were long enough with the program to get in good physical condition.[6]

However, Dr. Cooper's system is not one that can be carried out in ten minutes a day. He does not think much of the dynamic tension and isometric exercises. He advocates running, cycling, swimming, walking, and a long list of other types of sustained activity.

All of it is worked out on a point system so that you know when you are taking the right amount. You begin gradually and build up until you are exercising vigorously, for it is this type of exercise, sustained over a quite long period that does the trick of improving the entire circulatory system, and with it the rest of the body.

He emphasizes and re-emphasizes that heart patients and people with other physical disorders should consult with their physicians before beginning the Aerobics program.

It would be reasonable to assume that both the harmful tensions and the retardation of bodily functions that may accompany depression would tend to be largely counteracted by the exercise of the Aerobics or a similar program of regular and sustained exercise.

Exercise is relaxing and in such a way would help reduce unnecessary muscular tensions. Exercise is also stimulating and would certainly tend to counteract the sluggishness and retardation of physical processes accompanying the sagging mood.

Your Eating Habits May Help to Beat the Blues

Along with the right physical activities comes right eating as a factor in holding morale on a desirable level. There are numerous good books that give you the essentials of good diet. Among these I can recommend Catharyn Elwood's *Feel Like a Million* [7] (in paperback) and Dr. Roger Williams' *Nutrition in a Nutshell.*[8]

One need not become a food-faddist in order to find out what constitutes a diet that will give him the maximum of vitality and health, and keeps him at a desirable weight. Generally speaking, ample protein, fats, and carbohydrates (of the right kinds), minerals, and vitamins will achieve these ends.

Even among people with good incomes, it has been discovered that large groups in our nation are poorly nourished. Most of them do not eat enough of the right kinds of foods.

Depression might be due to faulty diet. With insufficient protein, vitality may be low. Vitamins are essential to our emotional and mental health. A number of years ago it was found out that too many patients were being admitted to mental hospitals from certain areas. It was discovered that the foods in these sections were deficient in niacin. These patients were confused, depressed, and some of them were subject to hallucinations and delusions.

When they were fed massive doses of niacin, they quickly lost their psychotic symptoms.

The eminent biochemist and nutrition expert Dr. Roger Wiliams states that "severe mental depression . . . can be brought about by nutritional deficiency. . . . Such cases have been almost miraculously cured within a period of 48 hours by the administration of the principal missing nutrient niacinamide." [9]

There are a number of controlled studies that verify the importance of well-balanced, adequate nutrition to emotional and mental health. For example, a deficiency of pantothenic acid was shown to result in symptoms of depression and apathy, as well as other disturbing physiological symptoms. [10]

Another such investigation studied the results of depriving a number of young men of the B-complex vitamins. The acute deficiency was followed by depression, anxiety, and generally increased emotionality. [11]

One of the most interesting studies was conducted during World War II with a group of young men placed on a semi-starvation diet of seventeen-hundred calories daily for three months. What resulted was a general breakdown of morale among these men. [12] They became moody, apathetic, and irritable. They lost interest in life and became unsociable. Most of them started the experiment with strong attachments to their girlfriends, and at the end of the experiment most of them had lost their girlfriends because they had also lost their interest in the opposite sex. The demoralization of this group was so complete that the investigators called it a "semi-starvation neurosis."

Problems of underweight and overweight also affect morale, and these problems are closely linked with diet. There can, of course, be other causes. It is easy to see that an unbalanced diet, or nutritional deficiencies, may be a factor in producing periods of depression.

Alcohol and the Blues

It is probably true that most alcoholics have some sort of basic and serious personality disturbance that makes them vulnerable to the excessive and too frequent use of alcohol. It is estimated that there are more than five million alcoholics in the United States, with an alarming increase exceeding what might be expected due to the simple factor of population increase.

The poorest imaginable prescription for counteracting the blues is to "drown your sorrows in drink." Temporarily the cortex is numbed and one may become less aware of his troubles for the time being. But the truth is that alcohol is a depressant. Imbibing considerable quantities of it will produce the blues instead of curing them. This may account for the low morale of millions of people who imbibe regularly and heavily.

How much can a person drink without serious depressing effects? I am not sure a pat answer is available. The human body can utilize only about one ounce of alcohol each hour, which is a very small amount.[13] When the alcohol content of the blood is as little as .1 per cent, the stage of intoxication is reached. At .5 per cent the drinker loses consciousness. When the amount reaches .55 per cent the person usually dies.

Recent medical research also indicates that alcohol has direct harmful effects upon the liver. In addition to all of these rather sobering facts, the person who drinks regularly many times loses his appetite for a well-balanced diet and usually begins to suffer from nutritional and vitamin deficiencies.

Your Physician May Prescribe Drugs That Will Help

If depression becomes too great for a person to cope with, he should consult with a competent physician who may be able to help in many ways.

In the first place a thorough medical examination may show whether the person has some physiological disorder that needs correcting. Also there are anti-depressant drugs that can certainly alleviate most depressions. These drugs must be prescribed and administered by a qualified physician. They will not cure depression, but they usually alleviate the worst of the symptoms.

Your Sleep Habits and the Blues

The average person needs from seven to eight hours sleep a night. There are many individual variations, of course.

Severe loss of sleep can result in depression, anxiety, and other psychological disturbances.[14]

It has been discovered that the need for sleep is associated also with a need for dreaming, which seems to be a necessity for mental, emotional, and physical well-being. Recent research has shown that everybody investigated has cycles of dreaming periodically during the night.[15] In the average night's sleep, there are usually four or five cycles of vivid dreams characterized by rapid eye movements during the dream. Even people who report that they never dream are found by laboratory investigation to have these periods of dreaming.

Loss of sleep can cause depression, but in turn depression can cause insomnia. Break the depression and you have better sleep habits. Establish better sleep habits and you may reduce depression.

There are many strategies for combatting both depression and anxiety. There are also strategies for counteracting insomnia. One of the simplest has been described in a former chapter—the skill of progressively relaxing the muscles of the body.

By using these practical strategies, a person should be able to enjoy a full night of sleeping. It is also reasonable to assume that right eating and right exercise have a bearing upon healthful sleeping.

We may conclude that reasonable health practices have an important bearing upon emotional and mental well-being. The human body is a wonderful self-repairing machine that functions splendidly if we give it a chance. Its harmonious functioning in turn helps produce and sustain positive attitudes and feelings.

---

[1] Shagass, Charles. "Explorations in the Psychophysiology of Affect," in J. M. Scher's (Ed.) *Theories of the Mind*. New York: The Free Press of Glencoe, 1962, pp. 122-132.

[2] Ruch, F. L. *Psychology and Life*. Chicago: Scott Foresman and Company, 1958, p. 151.

[3] Wolf, S. and H. G. Wolff. *Human Gastric Function, An Experimental Study of Man and his Stomach*. New York: Oxford Press, 1947.

[4] Cooper, K. H. *Aerobics*. New York: Bantam Books, 1968.

[5] *Ibid.*, p. 107.

[6] *Ibid.*, p. 144.

[7] Elwood, Catharyn. *Feel Like a Million*. New York: Pocket Books, 1965.

[8] Williams, Roger. *Nutrition in a Nutshell*. New York: Doubleday and Company, 1962.

[9] *Ibid.*, pp. 62-63.

[10] Dean, W. B., *et al.* "Pantothenic acid deficiency induced in human subjects." *Journal of Clinical Investigation*, 1955, 34, 1073-1084.

[11] Brozek, J., *et al.* "A study of personality of young men maintained on restricted intakes of vitamins of the B complex." *Psychosomatic Medicine*, 1946, 8, 98-109.

[12] Keys, A., *et al. The Biology of Human Starvation*. Minneapolis: University of Minnesota Press, 1950.

[13] Coleman, James C. *Abnormal Psychology and Modern Life*. Chicago: Scott Foresman and Company, 1964, p. 422.

[14] Noyes, A. P. and L. C. Kolb. *Modern Clinical Psychiatry*. Philadelphia: W. B. Saunders, 1963, p. 104.

[15] *Ibid.*, p. 104.

CHAPTER 16.

You Can Change Your Self-concept

How Do You Look at Yourself?

You CARRY AROUND with you in your thinking certain ideas about yourself. These ideas constitute your self-concept.

You have a certain concept of yourself as a swimmer. Perhaps after swimming for pleasure since childhood you recognize that you are an average swimmer, breaking no records, but doing pretty well at it and enjoying it.

On the other hand, you may know you are superior at bowling, or golf, or bridge, or fishing, or hunting. Perhaps you are even a local champion, and have sometimes felt you should attempt to compete in the big-time.

I know a man who feels he is intellectually adequate but socially inadequate. The way he defines himself has much to do with how well he performs in each of these activities.

In regard to all of our behavior we have formulated ideas about how well we do. Even about some things we have never tried, we think we might do well or poorly in them if we did try.

Self-concept Determines in Part How You Function

One of the important factors about self-concept is that it determines to a great extent how we function in certain areas of life.

For example, our friend who feels he is inadequate socially, may function inadequately primarily because he feels he has no capacity for social skills.

High school students who felt they were socially inferior have been given basic training in social skills. In nearly all cases, there was a great improvement in social functioning. The training did two things for them. First, it demonstrated to them that they could function successfully. Second, it showed them how to do so. The result was that these students began to see themselves in a new light, and they began to establish successful patterns of social behavior.

If you conceive of yourself as only an average swimmer, the probability is that you will never be more than an average swimmer. But if you conceive of yourself as a champion swimmer, the self-concept does not insure that you will become a champion. If you do not have the capacity for it, no amount of thinking you can be a champion will get you there.

But if you *have* the capacity, and do not conceive of yourself as superior, you will probably perform far below capacity. If you have the potential and *know* you have it, and *work* at achieving it, you can be rather confident of superior attainment.

We can take human subjects and hypnotize them and suggest to them that they are weak, and they will behave as weak people. This has been measured on the index of a machine measuring the strength of grip. Suggesting to subjects that they are very strong, the index for grip shoots up, even beyond the person's usual strength when not under hypnosis.

Does the suggestion give the subject superhuman grip? Not at all. It merely helps him to exert all the gripping strength he has.

In certain cases of emergency, some people will exhibit what seems to be superhuman strength. In this locality a frail woman, about middle-aged, lifted one section of an automobile under which her son was pinned. The strength was there all the time, but it was not mobilized and used to capacity. Of course, this type of exertion can be rather hard on a person who is not in good muscular condition.

Our attitude about our ability in any line has much to do with our performance. Many of our failures, our inefficiencies, are due to poor attitudes toward ourselves.

How Self-concept Is Formed

How do we come to have these attitudes toward ourselves? Many studies indicate that parental attitudes toward children have much to do with self-concept.[1] When a child is born, he has no self-concept. As he grows older, very slowly he begins to form some ideas about himself. Those ideas come about largely through the attitudes of his parents. If the child is treated as a person of worth, he begins to feel that way about himself.

In specific areas this sort of shaping or molding of self-concept takes place. I observed a three-year-old child drawing. She told her father, "Look, Daddy, I draw a man." The father hardly acknowledged that she was alive. He grunted and went on reading the paper.

The girl then turned to her mother, who said scornfully, "You call that a man? It looks more like hen-scratching to me. He's got no eyes nor mouth."

Rebuffed twice, the little girl turned away. If this sort of process was kept up, it would be easy to predict that her concept of herself as an artist would be very poor. Actually, for her age, her drawing was quite acceptable, for her man had a head and lumps that looked as if arms and legs were intended.

If this process goes on in many areas of a child's life, the child thinks less and less of himself. He begins to think of himself as a person who cannot do anything well. And he may get to the place where he will not even try to do things, feeling sure of failure. And failing to try things, he becomes apathetic, colorless, and uninteresting to himself and others.

Fortunately for some children, if their parents are constantly belittling them, others may help to correct their self-concept. An appreciative aunt, uncle, or neighbor may give the child's efforts some recognition, approval, or praise, and the child may begin to form a different picture of himself.

Under a wise and friendly schoolteacher, again, the concept may become more positive. Many a child with such a superior teacher has caught a vision of what he can achieve and what he can become.

If you have come this far in life with a negative concept of yourself, you are perhaps being cheated out of your birthright and all because of purely artificial barriers to achievement that have no basis in reality.

How You Can Improve Your Self-concept

You can develop a self-concept that will mean that you can come closer and closer to achieving your optimum in whatever potential you may have.

Most people are lacking in self-confidence. Such a lack may make you aim either too low or too high. We have recorded experiments that indicate this is usually the case with a person lacking in self-confidence.

Shooting too low may mean not trying to do anything at

all for fear of failure. Or it may mean trying something so far below your ability that you could not care less.

It is a good idea to begin with something at which you are pretty sure you can succeeed. If you have dramatic ambitions, start with a local drama in the church or the club. If this goes well try out for the local little theater or some similar amateur group.

Many times the person with dramatic ambition but little confidence wants to begin on Broadway or in Hollywood.

I have a young friend who has the ambition to become a writer. She also has above average ability. She started with something in which she was pretty confident of success— in the Sunday school magazines, in which her articles and stories are published regularly. Periodically she tries for something larger, and she may make the big-time someday. In the meantime, she is having fun, she is succeeding, she is rewarded financially, and has the great satisfaction of making a contribution to others.

So experiencing success may change your self-concept. However, there are other methods.

Practically everything you have read thus far in these chapters may be a means of bettering self-concept.

During the past several years, important research has been conducted regarding self-concept. Much of this was initiated by Dr. Carl R. Rogers and Dr. Rosalind Dymond of the University of Chicago, and a number of co-workers.[2] Both of the principal investigators are experts in counseling people who are maladjusted.

One previously known factor that was important in their

research was what is called the "ideal-self." The self-concept is the person you think and feel you are right now. The ideal-self is the person you would like to be, or the person you feel you ought to be.

These two concepts are sometimes rather far apart. Dr. Rogers and others had noticed that the farther apart the concepts were, the greater the maladjustment. That is, if the person you think you ought to be is a long way above what you think you are, you are likely to be an unhappy person. And the wider apart they are, the unhappier you are.

So they tested their observation out, measuring self-concept and ideal-self at the beginning and at the end of counseling. True to their predictions, counseling resulted in distinctly shortening the distance between self-concept and ideal-self. The person came to see himself much more the person he would like to be than before counseling. There is greater "self-understanding, increased inner comfort." And the person he wants to be is now a more realistic goal.

Several years following these original studies, two other investigators, Dr. A. E. Wessman of Dartmouth College and Dr. D. F. Ricks of Columbia University, undertook a somewhat similar study with students who were not maladjusted.[2] These studies dealt more with changes of mood from elation to depression or depression to elation in these well-adjusted students.

Here it was discovered that in periods of optimism, self-concept and ideal-self were much closer than in periods of depression. It was also discovered that the ideal-self varied little. The self-concept fluctuated considerably more.

What is there of practical value in these studies? One point is that you should be tolerant of your own failures and limitations. The old commandment is that we should love our neighbor as we love ourselves. We should have affection for ourselves, and not be self-condemning. An attitude of mercy and forgiveness toward oneself makes for strength. With such an attitude improvement becomes much more probable.

Another point that emerges is that you should keep your goals as realistic as possible. Expect of yourself what you can reasonably hope to achieve.

If your self-concept is too low, talk it out of your system. Verbalize what you think of yourself either orally or in writing. Get catharsis or release from these negative ideas about yourself.

When you have done this, begin with some affirmations that will gradually build your confidence in yourself. You will thus be conditioning yourself to have more confidence in your ability. You will begin to expect yourself to perform on a more significant level.

The general principle here is to free yourself from the wrong ideas of the past and their effects, and to set up a chain of new ideas, feelings, and actions that will mean betterment now and even more betterment in the future.

Positive experiences can help you build a positive self-concept. Begin with a task at which you know you can succeed. Repeat this success several times and let the confidence of success take hold of you. Increase the difficulty of the task slightly. Succeeding on lower levels builds confidence. Keep trying for slightly higher levels. Practice that at which you know you can succeed. As you increase the level of difficulty slowly, if you fail, return to the easier level for a time, and later try the higher level. Cultivate the habit of success.

[1] Baughman, E. E. and G. S. Welsh. *Personality, a Behavioral Science.* Englewood Cliffs, N. J.: Prentice-Hall, 1962, pp. 360-361.

[2] Rogers, C. R. and Rosalind Dymond. *Psychotherapy and Personality Change.* Chicago: The University of Chicago Press, 1954, pp. 413-434.

[3] Wessman, A. E. and D. F. Ricks. *Mood and Personality.* New York: Holt, Rinehart and Winston, 1966, pp. 23-32.

CHAPTER 17.

You May Get Help from Autosuggestion

THE WORD HYPNOSIS is frightening to some people. Even though frightened by it, most people are fascinated by the topic. There is nothing magical or mystical about hypnosis. It is a practical process that may sometimes achieve rather amazing results.

Because the word hypnosis may set up feelings that would constitute a barrier, I have preferred to use the word "suggestion." Hypnosis is a very strong type of suggestion and it involves the subject putting himself into a suggestible attitude.

There is a great deal written today about self-hypnosis or autohypnosis. Again let us recognize that the dividing line is very dim between autohypnosis and many suggestions you give yourself every day and carry through to completion.

Perhaps one of the differences has to do with the so-called trance-state. To achieve certain ends with autohypnosis apparently the trance-state is required. To achieve other ends a deep trance-state is needed. But most ends can be achieved with a very light trance-state.

Suggestion Without Trance

Also, I would not hesitate to say that most of the goals of self-improvement can be achieved without any trance at all. In fact there are many expert hypnotists that use what they call waking-hypnosis. And they get astounding results. They will tell their subjects, "You will remain wide awake and conscious of all that I say to you. You will remember all that happens here." And this is just the way it takes place.

Method for Autosuggestion

In the first method I am going to describe for self-improvement, you need not go into even a light trance. Let us call this method autosuggestion.

How can you give yourself suggestions that may lead to your betterment? How can you give yourself suggestions that may counteract those penalizing periods of depression and lift your morale?

It is advisable for you to find a place where you will be distracted as little as possible—a quiet private place in which no interruptions will take place.

Next it is advisable to recline comfortably. Stretch out on a bed or sofa or the floor or a bench or bare table. Then begin to relax yourself all over. Follow the Jacobson Progressive Relaxation method (see Chapter 2) or some similar method. If you have not had time to go into these methods, go over your body until you feel your arms, legs, stomach and back muscles, and those of face, scalp and neck are relaxed as well as you are able.

Next, tell yourself "You are going to be in a suggestible frame of mind. You are going to carry through with the suggestions I give."

Now give yourself some easy commands like "Clench your fist tight. Clench it tighter. Hold it tight. Now relax your hand. Completely relax it." You might do this with each hand.

Now repeat over to yourself, "You are very suggestible. You will carry out all suggestions I give you to their fullest. You will enjoy carrying out these suggestions. You will enjoy the results of carrying them out."

If you find yourself tensing up anywhere, relax. Go over your body to make sure you are completely relaxed.

Now begin with suggestions having to do with self-improvement. Have you been having difficulty meeting people? Suggest to yourself, "You will meet people with ease and enjoy meeting them. You will put them at their ease. You will become skilled in meeting people." It might be well for you also to picture yourself in the position of meeting people. You see yourself enjoying it and doing it well. And then it would be advisable to repeat these suggestions several times.

In raising your morale, give yourself the suggestions of goals you can achieve that bring you feelings of satisfaction. Repeat a general suggestion that you will find more each day to raise your spirits, to make you happy.

Whatever goal you wish to reach, return periodically to your state of relaxation and your attitude of suggestibility and repeat over to yourself the suggestions you wish carried out to attain these goals.

Many people find it very gratifying that these periods of autosuggestion are fruitful and bring dividends that are of great value. You will actually find yourself reaching your objectives.

It probably goes without saying that the goals you suggest should be attainable and realistic. Also these goals should be not only good for you but in no way harmful to anyone else. Preferably the blessings that come your way should be blessings for others at the same time.

This is one means of helping you fulfill your capacities. Very few of us are reaching self-fulfillment. We have great unrealized potential. Autosuggestion is one way to begin a life of self-fulfillment.

Autosuggestion and Autohypnosis

Dr. F. L. Marcuse, author of a good book on hypnosis, and a Fellow of the International Society for Experimental and Clinical Hypnosis, indicates that it is often hard to tell the difference between autosuggestion and autohypnosis.[1]

It would not be difficult to tell the difference between a deep-trance state necessary to achieve analgesia through autohypnosis, and the relaxed state of suggestibility described above as autosuggestion. Since, for the purposes of this chapter, no such deep-trance state is necessary, this distinction need not be experimented with at all.

Again there have been those who have advanced the opinion that the difference lies in the no-trance state of autosuggestion and the trance-state (even very light) of autohypnosis. But what is a trance?

Dr. Griffith Wynne Williams states that some degree of trance may take place in the course of many of our everyday activities—when one is motionless and quiet during fishing, or watching the fire in the fireplace.[2]

If by trance we mean a somnolent, relaxed, suggestible state, then we do have frequent trance-states. Dr. Williams, in the article in which he discusses this, is talking about "highway hypnosis," which is reported to be responsible for accidents. Keeping a constant visual stimulus—the stripe in the middle of the road, and the monotonous hum of the motor, and the relative immobility of the body, all seem to combine to lower a person's awareness, even if he is not asleep.

If this is a trance, then even during autosuggestion one may be in a light trance. For self-betterment in the general sense—to raise your morale, to give yourself more confidence, to help you do your work better—certainly one needs no deep trance.

Two Methods for Autohypnosis

One method for autohypnosis is similar to the one I have described above for autosuggestion. Dr. Robert W. White of Harvard says that nine out of ten methods for inducing hypnosis call for reclining posture, relaxation, and focusing the eyes on an object after which the eyes close.[3]

One hypnotist who sometimes uses autohypnosis goes through exactly the same routine with himself as with his subjects.

He lies prone in a place where he can be comfortable. He relaxes himself as completely as he can. Then he tells himself, "Now look steadily at that spot," (or nail, or whatever). "Your eyelids will begin to get heavy, very heavy. You will want to close your eyes. Your eyelids are getting very heavy. Now, close your eyes. You are now in a very suggestible state and you will follow my commands."

He then proceeds to give himself suggestions and usually they are very effective.

Autosuggestion or autohypnosis? What real difference does it make if it helps a person reach his worthwhile goals?

The second method is to go to an expert hypnotist who will give you post-hypnotic suggestions that on giving yourself a certain signal, you will go into a hypnotic trance during which you give yourself the desired suggestions.

For achieving the deeper trance-stages for something like anesthetizing a part of your body, this second method is perhaps more effective than the first.

Are There Dangers?

This is not an easy question to answer. The experts differ. Dr. Marcuse, cited above, says there is risk in self-hypnosis.[4] LeCron, on the other hand, in his widely read book on self-hypnosis, states there are no dangers.[5]

Certainly the process of autosuggestion as described above should carry with it no dangers at all, as long as you are suggesting something that will be good for you.

Using autohypnosis for anesthetizing portions of your body should be carried out only under medical supervision.

Also, I believe it would be safe to say that going to wild extremes with autohypnosis would be unwise. For example, people can self-induce hallucinations with autohypnosis. But why do it? What possible good can come from achieving such phenomena?

Autosuggestion and Positive Thinking

Autosuggestion does not differ very much from some of the techniques of positive thinking. In most of the positive-thinking methods you make affirmations. You repeat these to yourself frequently as you feel the need for them. This is a type of autosuggestion.

In the method of autosuggestion described here, progressive relaxation is a prerequisite. Many of the positive-thinking methods advocate the use of relaxation as beneficial, but it is usually not considered essential for the affirmations to do their good work.

Being able consciously to relax your entire body is a helpful process by itself. Autosuggestion requires as high a degree of concentration as you are capable of. You shut out distractions, including the distractions of unnecessarily tense muscles.

Also, with autosuggestion you put yourself in a suggestible frame of mind. So autosuggestion might be considered a special method of positive thinking.

It is well worth experimenting with. If you see that it pays dividends, there is no reason why you should not practice it as often as you need to.

---

[1] Marcuse, F. L. *Hypnosis, Fact and Fiction*. Baltimore: Penguin Books, 1961, p. 202.

[2] Williams, G. W. "Highway Hypnosis: An Hypothesis," *The International Journal of Clinical and Experimental Hypnosis*, 1963, 143-151.

[3] White, R. W. "A Preface to the Theory of Hypnotism," *Journal of Abnormal and Social Psychology*, 1941, 36, 477-505.

[4] Marcuse, F. L. *Op. cit.*, p. 12.

[5] LeCron, Leslie M. *Self-Hypnotism, The Technique and Its Use in Daily Living*. Englewood Cliffs, N. J.: Prentice-Hall, 1964.

CHAPTER 18.

Managing Your Fears

The Utility of Fear

You have perhaps read articles in which fear, anger, and sorrow are called "negative emotions." This description is not quite accurate. The basic behavior connected with each of these emotions has a positive value for the organism.

Fear has a survival value. You have a built-in mechanism that enables you to cope with emergencies. This mechanism gives you a burst of energy when you need it to escape from some actually threatening situation.

Briefly what happens is that your senses warn you of danger. The sensory message quickly goes to your brain. Your brain in turn sends messages speeding to other key parts of the body. The adrenal medulla reacts by injecting adrenalin into your bloodstream. Heart action speeds up.

196

Your liver turns glycogen loose into the bloodstream for quick energy. Your bronchial passages are dilated.

In short, your body is prepared for action. If this action is physical, it is usually to escape the threatening circumstances, which in this case are real, not imaginary. So fear has served you well and positively.

Not all fear is of the kind described above. Fear can become excessive and disorganizing. Fear can generalize from one situation to another to make you afraid unnecessarily. Suppose you were caught in a torrent of water and almost drowned. Later you could become afraid of all water, and that would be irrational.

Fear and Depression

Much sadness is caused by the actual loss of a valued object or person. If the loss is real, your sorrow is realistic. If the loss cannot be remedied, you grieve, and if you are wise, you go beyond your grief and try in any of several ways to make up the loss. If you lost a friend, you sorrow, and then find other friends.

Fear can quickly complicate the picture. I know parents who lost their first child. When a second child came, the loss of the first child made them irrationally afraid that they were going to lose the second. Instead of enjoying the second child to the fullest, they were constantly depressed at the thought of all the dire things that might happen to this one who was alive and well and happy.

A great deal of depression is connected with not what has been lost but what we fear may be lost. The fear of possible losses throws a blanket of gloom over us when we could be happy instead.

When fears of this kind become internalized and habitual, they are usually described as anxiety.

With these habitual fears, life becomes less joyful because the person is constantly fearful of what might happen or what might be lost. Now fear has become negative. It is not contributing to life but is subtracting from it. Fear of this kind has no usefulness, and has become a burden. It prolongs your sorrow unnecessarily, and magnifies it until it may color all of life.

What can we do about fears of this kind?

Recognize and Acknowledge Your Fear

Usually we are aware of being afraid. There are some rather subtle fears of which we are unaware, or only dimly aware. If we are to deal with fear intelligently, we must learn to recognize it when it is present.

What are examples of some of these fears that may pass unnoticed? Nearly always they are associated with a feeling of shame. For example, a high school girl was ashamed of what she called "buck teeth." Her teeth were not actually out of proportion, but she felt they were. This made her avoid situations in which she would laugh with her mouth open. She rationalized this by saying that, among other things, she thought high school boys were silly and for that reason, avoided their company.

She really wanted very much the company of high school boys, but her hidden fear made her avoid them. Then she became depressed because she was not sought after.

When she saw what her fear really was, and that it was irrational, and when she acknowledged it, her problem became much simpler.

Another example is that of a young man who saw his father die suddenly of a heart attack as he mowed the lawn. An experience of this kind is a terrific shock. There was no shame attached to this fear. For a long time this young man avoided any physical activity. He, too, would rationalize by saying the weather was too warm or that he was not feeling up to it.

He really enjoyed swimming and baseball and hard manual labor. Later when his own physician told him he needed more physical activity, and explained to him that this might even help prevent a heart attack, the whole problem came out in the open. Fortunately, this physician had also attended his father, and explained to him that one possible factor in his father's case was that he was unaccustomed to exercise and was not in good physical shape at the time of his death.

Fear can cheat you out of all sorts of interesting constructive experiences. Fear can make you feel weak and inadequate. Fear of failure can deprive you of the effort of trying to do something which might be very rewarding.

Two young men whom I know were on a fishing trip in the mountains with an older companion. They were caught in a sudden and violent electrical storm. The older man led them to a partially protected place where they waited the storm out. The electrical display was brilliant and accompanied by a deafening and incessant cannonade. One of the young men said to his older companion, "I don't see how you can be so calm."

He was greatly impressed when the older man answered, "I am terrified." Here was a simple, frank admission of fear under threatening circumstances over which they had little control.

Verbalize Your Fear

This older man was unashamed to admit his fear openly. He not only recognized it, and acknowledged it to himself, but acknowledged it without shame to others. This is one of the healthy ways of dealing with fear.

In the case of the high school girl mentioned above who was self-conscious, the girl felt free to talk about her problems with an understanding teacher. At first the girl said, "I don't like the boys here. They're so silly." She repeated this on several occasions.

Then one day she asked the teacher, "Did you ever notice my buck teeth?" The teacher truthfully said she hadn't. "Well," said the girl, "I have buck teeth and they make me very self-conscious."

In a later conference she said to the teacher, "I told you the boys here were silly. That really isn't true. I like them and admire them and want their company. But I've been self-conscious about my teeth and have been ashamed to laugh with my mouth open."

Verbalizing her fear, her self-consciousness, and her shame was a step toward overcoming her timidity and beginning to have a normal social relationship with boys.

Deal With the Source of Your Fear

Intelligent strategy in coping with fear would mean that you identify its source. Knowing clearly what you are afraid of and why is a big step toward overcoming fear.

If your fear is from some external threat, the job is much easier. I knew a young man who was afraid of swimming in deep water. He knew clearly what he was afraid of and remembered how it got started. At the age of six he jumped into deep water without knowing how to swim. He strangled and panicked and had to be rescued. Later he learned how to swim in shallow water but would never venture farther than waist-deep.

With the aid of an older friend he mapped a strategy whereby he overcame his fear and began enjoying swimming in deep water. He was attacking fear at its source.

There are external threats from which sometimes you have to escape. I have a friend who lived in a neighborhood in which his children were constantly threatened by gangs and individual hoodlums. There was no way he could change the entire area. When he had first moved into the community it was a law-abiding, good neighborhood. He had watched it slowly deteriorate and it continued getting worse. The only sensible thing for him to do was move.

There are fears which are much more subtle and difficult to deal with even if you identify them. Fear of death is an almost universal fear. Even here, acknowledging it and verbalizing might help to reduce its intensity.

There is a prominent comedian who says he laughs at death. When interviewed on the subject he said that he was a very religious man, had faith in a benevolent God, and believed that life was eternal and that what we call death is not the end of things in any sense of the word. Here is a person whose antidote to a universal fear was found in a comforting philosophy and religious belief. An accessible goal for each of us is to work out personal philosophies or religious beliefs that give us comfort and help in coping with the inevitable.

Get Into Action

One principle which seems broadly applicable in dealing with fear is to do something about it. Doing almost anything is usually better than doing nothing. When you get into action about your fear, nearly always fear is reduced quickly. When you are afraid, your body is readied for action; so get into action! You might need to escape and that is action. You might need to attack the source of your fear, and that, too, would be action.

Or even outlining for yourself a definite plan of coping with fear is a type of action. Putting the plan into effect would also be doing something about it.

A twelve-year-old boy discovered this principle when, due to circumstances beyond his or his parents control, he had to stay for several nights in a large house alone. The first night he went to sleep afraid but slept all night, anyway. The second night he awakened in the middle of the night, thought he heard strange noises in the house, and was petrified with fear. Finally, he worked up enough courage to turn on the light. He felt better, but he was still afraid.

He ventured into the next room and turned on the light. He proceeded to inspect every room in the house and having gone into action, and also having found nothing out of the ordinary, he was calmed enough to return to sleep. He realized that just getting into motion, doing something, served to reduce his fear. From experience he had learned a practical principle which he continued to apply from then on.

These are the practical strategies, then. Acknowledge your fear, verbalize it to some understanding person whom you can trust, try to remove the cause of your fear or remove yourself from the cause. And get into action.

Make the Action as Vigorous as Possible

Since fear prepares the body for action, vigorous action which would use the quick energy provided by fear would be effective in reducing fear. People who have suffered from stagefright have used this strategy successfully. Right before making the speech or taking part in the play, a long brisk walk reduces so-called "nervousness" and makes the person calmer and better organized. A good swim, a long bicycle ride, or game of tennis, or any of a dozen interesting physical activities would serve the same purpose.

As was pointed out in the chapter on exercise, people benefit psychologically in many ways from vigorous bodily activity, especially if it is engaged in regularly for rather protracted periods.

Initial Fear Is Reduced Through Experience

There are some fear-causing situations that should be avoided. Viewing a violent television program may make the viewer jittery and jumpy. What are you going to do with the physical by-products of fear after they have been produced?

On the other hand, many life situations which are unavoidable produce fear especially during the learning or initial stages. Many people experience fear of water as they learn to swim. Later, as one gains experience, the fear is displaced by pleasure. The same thing applies to driving a car.

I know an individual who has cheated himself out of many pleasurable experiences because he let fear conquer him as he first tried to drive a car. Now, as an adult, he must depend upon other people to transport him.

On the other hand, another man I know was extremely fearful for a long time as he learned to speak in public. Later he came to enjoy the stimulus of making a public address.

As a person gains skill, he grows less fearful. As with so many other processes, there is an interaction taking place. As he loses his fear, he gains in skill. The activity becomes less fearful, he becomes more confident, and the really tension-producing fear may be lost altogether.

Determination May Be Half the Battle

If you are the victim of fear, your determination to overcome it will lead you to the strategy or strategies that will help you overcome fear.

The outstanding writer Lew Sarrett used to tell how he overcame fear. Believing himself to be an unusually fearful person, he placed himself in situations which were fearful for him, knowing that only through facing these, could he overcome his fear. He told of his irrational fear of snakes and how he made himself walk in the woods and fields and have encounters with snakes until he was no longer fearful. His determination to conquer fear was the attitude that made the difference.

The final encouraging word here is that fear can be dealt with intelligently and successfully. If it occurs, its effects can be directed wisely. If it is now conquering you, you can conquer it. You can in this respect be the master. You can have the sense of controlling your own life rather than letting circumstances control you.

CHAPTER 19.

Managing Your Anger and Hostility

Most of the authorities in the field of mental health agree that one of the greatest sources of personality disturbance lies in the way the individual fails to manage his hostility intelligently. If a person represses hostility, eventually it will find its way out, sometimes in surprising directions. Or he may take his hostility out on himself. Again many of the authorities agree that in such a case of intropunitiveness, the person may become quite depressed.

As with fear reactions, not all anger reactions are negative. Some of them apparently have a survival value for the organism. The African lion will usually run away from hunters. We call this a fear reaction in which the behavior is escape from danger. If the hunter persists in his pursuit of the lion with the animal fleeing and taking cover repeatedly, eventually there will be an anger or a rage reaction.

The hunted animal evidently sees that the only way he can cope with the threat of the hunter is to attack. He does this as a matter of survival.

There are parallels in human life in which a person is threatened in some way by others and eventually may attack the source of the danger. There are instances of groups of people who tired of corruption in government and became angered and threw out the corrupt officials, replacing them with new people who promised more integrity in government.

This is what has sometimes been called "righteous indignation," which is an intelligent directing of anger reactions against a source of threat to remove it. Apparently this is a healthy, wholesome type of behavior, resulting in the betterment of man's condition.

In its physiology, anger is similar to fear but with certain differences. In fear, adrenalin is dominant as a hormone touching off certain physical mechanisms. In anger there is adrenalin but also noradrenaline, which seems to be the dominant hormone. Activity of the heart is even greater in anger than in fear, depending somewhat on the degree of the emotion. Blood pressure is usually higher in anger than in fear. Physiologically, the anger reaction is our most violent automatic reaction.

How does anger relate to the blues? Already mentioned

above is the intropunitive reaction in which the person takes his anger out on himself. He could do this for many apparent reasons. He might be angry at himself because of his mistakes and failures, for example. But many times intropunitiveness is a guilt reaction. He blames himself for many things and seeks to punish himself to alleviate his guilt. Most of us are taught in childhood not to be angry with Mother, Father, or other members of the family. But most of us normally experience anger toward parents or brothers and sisters. While we may not openly express this anger, nevertheless, the anger is there. Then we feel guilty about it, and if the guilt feelings are strong, we believe that we are unworthy, terrible people to be angry with those we are supposed to love.

Or these suppressed feelings of anger may break through causing us to say and do things we are deeply ashamed of afterwards. Again, we are experiencing guilt reactions that cause us to be depressed because we see our attitudes and behavior as reprehensible.

One point needs clearing up here. People must learn to inhibit violent behavior when they experience anger toward others. Otherwise anarchy would reign. There was a trend twenty or thirty years ago that said, "No inhibitions. Inhibitions are harmful. Let yourself go. Do anything you feel like doing." I do not know any serious students of human behavior that presently advocate this.

True, Dr. Salter advocates the disturbed individual putting aside most inhibitions and behaving spontaneously.

But Dr. Salter is addressing himself to the habitually *over*-inhibited, in an attempt to help them regain some balance away from an extreme position.

All of us must learn to suppress anger responses. We must learn when it is inappropriate and ineffective to express anger even in words.

What then constitutes a healthy management of anger and hostility? First, if you suppress it, recognize it for what it is. You admit to yourself you are angry, even if you are not expressing it. Your expression of it is delayed, but you know you will later express it.

If expressing your anger verbally at the moment is inappropriate or unwise, later you can blow off steam and tell some understanding friend how you felt. You should have a friend you can talk to in the plainest or the most graphic language. In this way you acknowledge your anger; you express it fully without hurting yourself or anyone else.

One type of delayed expression we must avoid is what is called "taking it out on someone else." The professional word for this is "displacement" of anger. Eventually this causes a great deal of trouble for both the angry person and the target of his anger. A large percentage of all the trouble we experience in society is due to this behavior pattern of "taking it out on someone else."

Instead we can always verbalize our anger. We can tell it to someone who will understand. We can sometimes sit down and write about it and get release. Or again we can express it in art forms such as drawing, painting, music, or poetry.

Since the body is readied for action by anger, one of the most helpful ways of reducing it is through competitive games. A friend of mine has frequently said that he gets rid of a great deal of his pent-up hostility by hitting the golf-ball a resounding whack and sending it speeding down the fairway.

A vigorous swim, a long walk, jogging, bicycle riding, tennis, or any of a hundred wholesome physical activities help people work off their anger.

Another point needs clearing up. In everyday social relations there comes a time—perhaps infrequently—when someone needs telling off. If you and others have been frequently taken advantage of, or exploited, or imposed upon, there comes a time when you may have to speak out in anger. This is akin to the righteous indignation spoken of above. But here we are thinking more about what happens in private life, such as in the home.

Sometimes a husband may take unfair advantage of his wife, or she of him. Just so much of this is all most people ought to take. Speaking out clearly, bluntly, firmly, and courageously is an emotionally healthy thing to do. And it is wholesome for the relationship, too. No one should allow himself to be exploited.

Of course, such an outburst of anger should be followed by intelligent discussion to iron out inequities. Perhaps intelligent discussion beforehand could have prevented the outburst. Clear communication should exist in all human relations and can prevent a great deal of trouble.

There is still another facet to this subject. Some of us

are hypersensitive. Others appear threatening to us when they really are not. Situations appear threatening when they are not. Anger in such cases is irrational and inappropriate.

As we begin to live more realistically and to gain more satisfactions out of life, we should see that many situations we appraised as threatening are really not at all. A person may make a casual remark that is harmless and yet we misinterpret it as a very personal attack.

As one learns to solve his own problems, external situations which before aroused either fear or anger now only appear for what they really are: problems to be solved. An attitude of realism, of objectivity, will gradually cut down on the harmful side of emotionality.

The method of verbal self-conditioning would apply to many of the problems connected with anger and hostility. Verbal affirmations can reduce anger. The rational processes can influence the emotions and these rational processes are usually couched in language. Our "internalized self-talk" can reduce both fear and anger. Repeated affirmations of good will and confidence toward others will help offset anger.

In summary, the intelligent management of all the excesses of negative emotions would follow certain guidelines:

1. Acknowledge and admit the presence of the emotion.

2. Verbalize it fully to some understanding person in whom you can place confidence, or write how you feel fully—or do both.

3. Counteract the physical aspects of the emotion by some vigorous and, if possible, enjoyable activity.

4. Be as objective and realistic as possible about the cause or causes of the emotion, and do as much as you can to either eliminate the cause or reduce it.

5. Consciously set up habitual processes of positive thought to take the place of the negative thinking that sustains and accompanies the negative emotions.

The fact is that you can manage effectively and creatively your emotional life. You can sustain positive thought and emotions and patterns of behavior habitually. This, of course, means for you a happier and more successful life, which is your human heritage.

CHAPTER 20.

The Examples of Noted People May Help You Beat the Blues

TODAY WE HAVE DISCOVERED a great deal about maintaining high morale. This knowledge comes from a number of sources. Keeping morale high when things are going smoothly is in itself an achievement, but what about holding it up under the most trying conditions?

A great deal of this latter knowledge comes from the military. As much as we deplore war and hold out hope that the human race will abolish it forever, we have learned about the behavior of men under threat by keeping records of men during combat.

The greatest number of breakdowns in the military occurred in men who were immature, usually due to maternal

214

overprotection.[1] The greatest resistance to breakdown was in men with adequate personality integration.

Good group identification made for high morale. If the men in the group were friendly with each other and there was group cohesion or solidarity, morale tended to remain high.

Another outstanding factor was whether the man in combat knew why he was fighting, what he was fighting for, and was convinced that the war goals were right.

Activity was another key to morale. During periods of inactivity, morale tended to sag. When the men were busy, their spirits were better. The two cases that follow are those of people who, under the most trying conditions, managed to remain courageous, strong, and resistant to depression.

The Inspiring Example of Johnny Gunther

The heroic story of Johnny Gunther has been beautifully and movingly told by his father, John Gunther, the widely known author, in a small volume entitled *Death Be Not Proud*.[2] I recommend it heartily with no reservations. What I shall have to say here is in no way a substitute for the total impact of this book about which William L. Shirer wrote, "What a tribute to the fortitude, the beauty, and the invincibility of the human spirit." [3]

When Johnny Gunther was sixteen, about to graduate from Deerfield Academy, he became the victim of a brain tumor which later became malignant. Surgery revealed that the tumor had already grown to the size of an orange and was so deeply embedded that it could not all be removed without the operation causing death.

As it turned out, two difficult operations were performed. During one period of a rather unorthodox therapy, Johnny seemed to improve; then he became worse, and died of hemorrhage after an illness of fifteen months.

Johnny was not given to periods of depression prior to the onslaught of his fatal illness. But how he sustained high morale with hardly a break in the face of his fatal illness is one of the most remarkable achievements ever recorded. In spite of progessive physical deterioration during almost the entire fifteen months, his spirits remained high, and he was generally cheerful, optimistic, and thoughtful of others. How did he do it? Perhaps there are several outstanding factors.

One of these was the remarkable love and understanding of both of his parents, each of whom played a distinct role in helping their son during this indescribably trying ordeal. He frequently confided in his mother. Communication with her about his feelings, his plans, his hopes, and his brief periods of black despair helped to dispel that despair and replace it with courage and cheer.

While Johnny Gunther had nothing to do with having such fine parents whom he could trust and in whom he could confide, friendship is a gift that each of us can provide for himself. Love begets love. Friendship is responded to with friendship. We can find friends whose love and understanding can make a great deal of difference during our times of trouble.

Johnny Gunther was a boy who had developed many interests. He did not allow these diverse interests to flag during his illness, except when he was temporarily disabled by operations. He loved collecting interesting rocks and was a student of geology. He kept working at this.

He delighted in playing chess and kept it up, too, all during his illness. He enjoyed reading and being read to, and he was interested in mathematics and physics and read and studied these subjects.

He kept planning ahead. He was determined to graduate from Deerfield. His major interest and concern was his school work and he worked at it persistently. And graduate he did. At the time he had a great hole in his skull, covered by a flap of skin. He was barely able to walk. His left arm and hand were almost disabled. But he walked across the platform and received his hard-earned diploma.

His father wrote that the applause that spontaneously arose was like a storm. It was thunderous.

How did Johnny Gunther sustain high morale under circumstances that would have sunk most people under a morass of depression? Through loving companionship with his parents, through thoughtfulness of others, through a breadth of interests and activities which he sustained in the face of an uncertain future. And through it all, he kept a saving sense of humor. Life was a serious matter, death was near; but his unfailing good humor rose above all of it.

The Courage of Viktor Frankl

Dr. Viktor Frankl is an eminent Austrian psychiatrist, lecturer and writer. He is a professor of neurology and psychiatry at the University of Vienna Medical School. During World War II he became the victim of the Nazi persecution of the Jews and spent about three years in Auschwitz, Dachau, and other concentration camps.

How he suffered and survived these privations is told in his book *From Death Camp to Existentialism.*[4] In this book he does not magnify the horrors and agonies of his imprisonment. He gives brief accounts that furnish samples of the ordeals through which he passed. Much is left unsaid as the author leaves to the reader's imagination the magnitude of his unparalleled deprivation and suffering.

How in such unspeakable circumstances did he keep himself from complete suicidal hopelessness? How did he manage not to surrender to feelings of despair and futility that would have resulted in his being overwhelmed by the living death through which he was passing? Hundreds of fellow-prisoners committed suicide by hurling themselves against the electrified fences. Hundreds died because they lost hope. Yet Viktor Frankl managed to come through his valley of the shadow a stronger man than he had ever been.

First, he was sustained by the love he had for his wife and family and by the knowledge of their love for him. He says, ". . . love is the ultimate and the highest goal to which man can aspire. . . . The salvation of man is through love and in love."

He describes one cold morning when under the curses and blows from the rifle-butts of his captors, the prisoners were driven stumbling and starved to their heavy manual labor.

Frankl was sustained by the image of his wife: "I heard her answering me, saw her smile, her frank and encouraging look . . . more luminous than the sun which was then beginning to rise.

"I understand how a man who has nothing left in this world, still may know bliss, be it only for a brief moment, in the contemplation of his beloved."[5]

Second, life, even in the concentration camps, held deep meaning for him. The future held meaning for him and he planned for the future. Suffering held meaning for him, for it called forth courage, and since it was, at the time, his destiny to suffer, the way he bore the burden of suffering was an opportunity to draw on his courage.

Third, he kept his inner freedom—"the last of the human freedoms—to choose one's attitude in any given set of circumstances." [6] And this last freedom can never be taken away from any man.

Fourth, he was constantly trying to alleviate the sufferings of his fellow-prisoners, both psychologically and physically.

Fifth, he had a sustaining faith in God. Brought back

from a distant work-site, tired, hungry, and cold, he and his fellow-prisoners would gather for prayer in the corner of their hut.

Two Famous Men Who Conquered Serious Depressions

In a previous chapter it was mentioned that the great Mahatma Gandhi counteracted his spells of depression by reciting to himself selected verses from the Hindu scriptures in the Bhagavad Gita. He testified that he could very quickly and successfully change his emotion from negative to positive, from depressed to confident, by this simple method.

The examination of the methods used by other noted people may give you ways of dealing with periodic depression. It may also give you confidence that depression *can* be dispelled and that a person can consciously overcome defeating pessimism and maintain a healthy optimism.

DR. WILLIAM JAMES, PHILOSOPHER AND PSYCHOLOGIST

The depressions of Gandhi appear to have been fairly mild and infrequent, notwithstanding the adversities he suffered and the fact that he was frequently thwarted in achieving his goals.

The depressions of William James were of a more

serious order. As a boy, he was witty, cheerful, and active. However, when he was in his late twenties, he began to suffer from periodic spells of depression.[7] These continued for several years. His improvement was gradual. Even after he was emotionally stabilized and could be said to have conquered the worst of his depressions, they continued to recur periodically. But he had learned to cope with it and could pull himself out.

Just when his most serious attacks occurred we are not sure. This one he described later as a case study in *Varieties of Religious Experience*.[8] The onslaught of this early episode was sudden, ". . . there fell upon me without any warning, just as if it came out of darkness, a horrible fear of my own existence." There arose in his mind the memory of a patient he had seen in a mental hospital. "This image and my fear entered into a species of combination with each other. That shape am I, I felt, potentially. . . . There was such a horror of him that . . . I became a mass of quivering fear. After this the universe was changed for me altogether. I awoke morning after morning with a horrible dread . . . a sense of the insecurity of life that I never knew before. . . . It gradually faded, but for months I was unable to go out into the dark alone."

One can see the severely disturbing nature of these attacks of anxiety and depression. How did William James cope with it? He fell back upon religious belief. He wrote, ". . . the fear was so invasive and powerful that if I had not clung to scripture texts like 'The eternal God is my refuge,' etc., 'Come unto me, all ye that labor and are heavy-laden,' etc., 'I am the resurrection and the life,' etc., I think I should have grown really insane."

William James had also been bothered by a problem in philosophy, a very old one, concerning the question of determinism and free will. Is everything worked out in advance by forces over us which we have no control, or can man in some measure decide his own fate?

For William James this was no purely theoretical question. It was a matter affecting him personally. Was there something he could do about his own condition? Or was it fixed and predetermined?

He was helped in the resolution of this difficulty by an essay written by the French philosopher, Renouvier.[9] James wrote, "I . . . saw no reason why his definition of free will —'the sustaining of a thought *because I choose to* when I might have other thoughts'—need be the definition of an illusion. . . . My first act of free will shall be to believe in free will." He determined to do more, be more active, and engage in less introspection. This feeling that he could do something about his condition raised his morale considerably.

Later William James came to a clear-cut conclusion that mental disorder need not have a physical basis, that the mind could act without coercion from the body. Again he was uplifted by the feeling that he could in large measure control his mental processes.[10] He had also discovered that what *he believed* had much to do with how well he digested his food, how well he slept, and how well he felt. He knew it worked the other way around, too.

We find him then advocating what he called "the religion of healthy-mindedness," which has much in common with the morale-building New Thought groups and the power of positive thinking. At one time Dr. James went for "treatment" to a New Thought practitioner and was enthusiastic in his praise of her effectiveness.

There is no question that his marriage to a loving, stable young woman, Alice Gibbens, helped to offset his depressive tendencies. Also, his finding the vocation for which he was best suited—teaching—upgraded his morale.

William James in his twenties was emotionally disturbed, anxious, depressed, and suicidal. Yet he overcame this and became a dynamic teacher, writer, lecturer, and influential world citizen, as well as a good father and husband.

The factors leading to his self-improvement could be listed this way:

1. Recourse to help from religion, including repeated affirmations of comforting verses of scripture, and later practicing "the religion of healthy-mindedness."

2. Working out a satisfactory *personal* philosophy leading to action, achievement, and a feeling that he was to a great extent master of his own life.

3. Marriage to a loving, stable woman.

4. Finding a satisfying career.

There were many other elements relating to his change.

He had many wonderful friends and a very understanding younger brother (Henry) in whom he could confide. He had frequent diversions of travel and took vacations when he needed them. He had a wide variety of interests, all the way from gardening to psychic research.

One question that may confront us here is whether men of high level intellegence such as William James are more subject to emotional and mental disturbance than other people. The answer to this, on a basis of percentages, is that the highly intelligent are no more prone, and may be even less prone, to emotional-mental disturbances than the person with average intelligence.

LEO TOLSTOY, ONE OF THE WORLD'S GREAT WRITERS

Tolstoy at an early age became a successful writer. He had a sense of the artistic and an insight into human nature and behavior. He owned a large estate, the royalties from his writings were bountiful, and he had an affectionate wife and children.

But here was a man who could not be satisfied with what most people think would make them happy (although whether it actually would is dubious). Leo Tolstoy was always asking himself "Why?" [11]

What was the meaning of life and of his work? What was the meaning of his success? Did it all add up to nothing when death intervened?

As Tolstoy matured, these and similar questions became more and more insistent. As they did, he became more and more depressed. Finally his depression became so serious that he found himself no longer able to work. His work, indeed his entire life, seemed to have lost their meaning.

One of his brothers died quite young and Tolstoy later said, ". . . he died without understanding why he had lived, and still less what death meant to him."

As he approached middle-life, Tolstoy found his depression growing worse. He frequently experienced periods of deep perplexity when he could not work and could only ask the question "Why?"

He became convinced that these were not passing periods, but were serious and that he would have to find answers to his questions before he could improve.

Tolstoy wrote that not knowing the why of life blocked him completely, virtually shutting him off from life. He felt that the very earth on which he stood was falling to pieces. His life had no stable foundation. What he had lived for previously was meaningless, and now he had no reason to live. Thus while he continued to exist, to sleep, breathe, eat, and move, life had really come to a halt. The fulfillment of none of his past desires now seemed reasonable.

In the midst of this growing depression, in which life appeared to have no meaning, he began to entertain notions of suicide. He said he did not want to kill himself. He was afraid of death. Yet as he confronted a life that held for him no meaning, death was the logical solution. Eventually life became so fraught with fear, disappointment and bitterness that he was ready to kill himself to be liberated from his horror. But he also felt a horror of what awaited him after death, and that it might be even more horrible than his depressed condition, but said he could not wait patiently for natural death.

In the midst of these despairing thoughts and feelings, he had the thought that it was possible he had missed something in the accumulated knowledge of the world that might be of help to him.

This was the beginning of a diligent search into every branch of knowledge. But an extensive survey yielded nothing that was of value to him.

Having failed to find help in the available knowledge of the world, "I began to seek it in life itself." He began to watch the life of the masses of common people. It seemed that many of them had found a meaning in life.

This meaning in life came through a belief in God. He admitted that beyond mere logic and reasoning, there was another knowledge—faith—which could give meaning to life.

After a great deal of this sort of thinking, he reported that "I was now ready to accept any faith that did not require of me a direct denial of reason. He began a thoughtful study of Buddhism, Mohammedanism and especially Christianity.

In this quest he found himself drawn more to simple people, the peasants, the pilgrims and the monks. Also he came to the conclusion that a man must labor, not for himself alone but for all.

The simple thought of God's existence was enough to start life flowing through him afresh and to restore joy. He said he lived only when he felt faith in God. When he forgot God it was equal to death. Feeling a consciousness of God and seeking him meant that Tolstoy really felt alive. He began to realize that God and life were the same thing. Now he found his depression lifted and life rising up within and around him. The light shining within him never again left him. All the radiance and power of life returned to him.

The major part of his battle against a serious depression was won. He tried to return to his childhood church, but found too much that he could not accept or believe. Gradually he evolved his own rational faith and to live accordingly.

Even after this his life was filled with turbulence. He was repelled by the values of the people of his social class, and could not refrain from showing it. Now he tried to use his superb ability in writing to better the condition of mankind. This frequently brought him into conflict with his culture, including the government, and perhaps, most disturbing of all—his own family who were at first not in sympathy with his beliefs and practices.

His new-found faith also led him to behavior that was looked upon as strange and irrational. He began working to improve the lot of the Russian peasant. He dressed as a peasant and went for long periods living the austere life of a peasant, doing manual labor, eating simply and renouncing the luxuries of wealth.

He was never again plagued with the question of the meaning of life. He lived a life of love and service and as an aged man reported that this belief and this way of life had given him an unshakable tranquility.

The method Tolstoy had found for himself that overcame his serious, deep-seated depression was a simple one: (1) faith in God; (2) return to the essentials of primitive Christianity; and (3) a life of service and love to better the condition of his fellow-beings.

Discussion

These two examples of Dr. William James and Leo Tolstoy have been presented here to give encouragement to all people who suffer from periods of depression. If these seriously disturbed men could find their way through the maze of bafflement, frustration, and feelings of futility, surely the normal person with a less serious disturbance can also find a way to counteract his periods of depression.

Neither of these men received psychiatric or psychological treatment. Neither really had the chance. William James met Sigmund Freud long after the American philosopher and psychologist had resolved his major emotional and mental difficulties.

Certainly no one will draw the conclusion that those who have serious disturbances do not need professional help. They do, and should be helped to find it as early as possible. But it is encouraging to know that even without professional help, both of these men, using means that are today accessible to everyone, overcame their difficulties and lived long useful lives after they had found the way.

The following chapter is written in the hope that anyone

who reads it who has deep-seated, prolonged depressions will recognize the difficulty early and seek professional medical help which can make a great difference in his life.

[1] Coleman, James C. *Abnormal Psychology and Modern Life.* Chicago: Scott, Foresman and Company, 1962, p. 173.
[2] Gunther, John. *Death Be Not Proud.* New York: Pyramid Books, 1949.
[3] *Ibid.*, front cover.
[4] Frankl, Viktor. *From Death Camp to Existentialism.* Boston: The Beacon Press, 1959.
[5] *Ibid.*, pp. 36-37.
[6] *Ibid.*, p. 65.
[7] Perry, R. B. *William James.* New York: George Braziller, Publisher, 1954.
[8] James, William. *Varieties of Religious Experience.* New York: The Modern Library, 1902, pp. 156-158.
[9] Allen, G. W. *William James.* New York: Viking Press, 1967, p. 168.
[10] *Ibid.*, pp. 179-180.
[11] Tolstoy, L. N. *My Confession.* New York: Charles Scribner's Sons, 1917, p. 10.

CHAPTER 21.

Knowledge of the More Serious Types of Depression May Be Helpful

DEPRESSION SOMETIMES BECOMES EXTREME. Even people who do not have much insight into their moods may effectively overcome the usual type of depression. Common sense would direct the person to get his mind off himself and his troubles, to become active, and to seek the pleasant company of friends.

Sometimes a depression will get out of hand and seem to be beyond the common-sense methods of control. Even those serious depressions fall into different categories of serious-ness. Broadly speaking, we can divide them into three categories: reactive depressions, neurotic depressions, and psychotic depressions. There is not complete agreement even on this simple classification. Some authorities classify the reactive and neurotic both under the heading of neurotic. However, for the purposes of our discussion, we will discuss the three categories named.

Reactive Depression

This depressive condition is due to circumstances that can be identified. The person has lost someone very dear and necessary to him. He may have had serious business reverses or disappointments. He may have had any of a great variety of frustrations. Or he may have had a combination of depressing circumstances. But these are identifiable. He can tell you how he happened to get into this extended period of depression.

The difference between this and the normal sort of depression any person may have is that in this case the victim does not snap out of it. His depressed mood is severe and prolonged.

If he sees this is happening, he should seek help either from his physician, a psychiatrist, or a competent clinical psychologist. The advantage of going to an M.D. is that sometimes one of the simple chemotherapeutic drugs may be prescribed. Usually, it is one of several antidepressants, or a combination antidepressant and tranquilizing drugs. The doctor might also give some psychological help, depending on what kind of a doctor he is. If he is a psychiatrist, naturally he could and would give psychological help as well as possible chemotherapeutic help.

The clinical psychologist could give psychological help and might refer the depressed person to an M.D. for possible chemotherapeutic assistance.

The Neurotic Depression

In this case, we may find two sets of factors: (1) a setback of some kind from environmental sources, (2) complications because of certain personality traits or tendencies.

In one sense this type of depression is like the reactive depression, but in another sense it is different. There are identifiable setbacks, or frustrations, or sorrow from the environment. But there are also internal attitudes, feelings, and ideas that make the depression more difficult to deal with.

If the person who has had the disappointments, sorrows, or other setbacks begins to blame himself excessively, experiences severe guilt feelings in connection with failure, or feels that he has been negligent or remiss in his duty, the entire situation becomes more complex.

For example, a man has had a business failure. He is disappointed and sad because he failed. Then he begins to accuse himself of being a poor husband, a poor father, and a poor provider for his family. Now we not only have sadness because he failed in business. We have sadness because of deep personal shame, deep feelings of guilt, and sometimes an angry self-condemnation.

Imagine a mother whose child has died. There would be normal grieving and weeping. But suppose she begins to tell herself, "Surely I am to blame for my child's death. There must have been something I could have done that I did not do."

Perhaps she did everything she could do, and still her child died. Even in this case she may think, "I am surely to blame. God is punishing me by taking my child. If I were not such a terrible person, God would not have punished me this way. I am guilty of the death of my child."

The authorities say that there are two sources for the neurotic depression: (1) exogenous, that is, originating from the outside; (2) endogenous, originating from within.

What other symptoms, other than feelings of dejection, discouragement, and self-condemnation, might be present in a neurotic depression? There would also be feelings of hopelessness and futility. Sometimes there is a feeling of apathy and a lack of interest in others and in normal activities. There may be vague feelings of discomfort, headaches, and a variety of bodily complaints. Insomnia may increase a tendency to be depressed; or depression may cause insomnia— the beginning of a "vicious cycle." Most of the clinicians report the insomnia of depression characteristically to be an awakening unusually early in the morning, with the inability to go back to sleep. Also, there may be difficulty in concentrating.

If the depression is the reactive type without the endogenous factors, usually the person will recover much more quickly. If the endogenous factors are present, the recovery will take longer.

Even with the presence of endogenous factors, sometimes the person will recover without professional help, as in the case of William James.

Certain personality types seem to be more subject than others to the endogenous depressions. Usually the personality is characterized by rigid conscience development and a tendency to be introverted.

The victim of either the exogenous or endogenous depression, or a combination, usually knows that he is overreacting to the situation, but he may not know why this is so.

The sane procedure in the case of any prolonged depression is to seek professional help. Merely going to a professional person and telling him about the depression is in itself helpful. Sometimes, after a few conferences, the depressed person finds he has snapped out of it and is his normal self again.

If the neurotic depressive becomes suicidal, the physician may want his patient hospitalized for a short time for his own protection. The suicidal depressive should not resent this course of action, since it is a safeguard against possible tragedy.

Depressions Classified as Psychotic

The word insane is now an outdated word used only in legal terminology. A person who is mentally ill is correctly called psychotic.

There are several types of depressions which are classified as psychoses.

For all of the critical depressions the prognosis is generally good. A large percentage of these depressives recover and return to normal life.

What is the difference between the depressions classified as psychotic and those classified as neurotic? Some of the symptoms are similar but much more severe in the psychosis.

Most physicians would wish for a psychotic patient to be hospitalized almost without exception. This facilitates treatment and reduces the danger of suicide.

One of the most common of these psychoses is called manic-depression. In the manic phase, if it occurs, the person is usually overactive and elated. In the depressed phase, the patient is dejected, uncommunicative, and inactive.

Some of the manic-depressives have extreme swings of mood. The person may be elated, overactive, and even violent, and then fall into the deepest imaginable depression suddenly, refusing to communicate, appearing to be extremely dejected. Or it may happen the other way around—from an extremely depressed mood to the excitability of the manic phase. Some have only the depressed phase without the manic. A few are manic with no descent into depression.

The symptoms in the manic phase are those of accelerated muscular activity, accompanied by loud talking. The person usually moves rapidly and talks rapidly. He seems to have unbounded energy and enthusiasm, and is easily distracted. He may have grandiose delusions imagining himself to be a scientific genius or a great religious leader who is about to save the entire world. He may become violent and destructive. In his peaks of excitability and destructiveness, he may sometime become dangerous to those near him.

In the depressed phase the patient may feel lonely and abandoned by all his friends. He is sad and hopeless. His world is one of despair. He feels that he is a terrible person, the world's worst sinner. He may even believe that he has committed the "unpardonable sin" and has been abandoned by God. He suffers from feelings of deepest guilt, usually without knowing specifically what he feels guilty about. He may communicate in monosyllables or even refuse to communicate at all.

He becomes inactive and if he moves, he does so very slowly. His ideas seem to be retarded, and when he talks, speech is also painfully slow.

He may have delusions about his body, feeling that he is rotting internally, or that some vital organ has been severed or is missing. Hallucinations, both visual and auditory, may take place during manic-depression.

In the two extremes of swings of mood, there are degrees of disturbance. In the manic, one may be in the less violent hypomanic stage in which he exhibits certain amount of control, but with excitability, great energy, little need for sleep, and laying plans on a grand scale. The upper extreme is the delirious mania, in which the patient becomes incoherent and disoriented. His physical activity ascends to a feverish pitch, with endless rapid pacing, wild screaming, singing, gesticulating, and shouting.

Depressions vary also. The mildest is the simple type, during which the patient has clear memory, good orientation, and answers questions rationally. The lowest extreme is the depressive stupor, when he becomes almost totally unresponsive, refuses to eat, is completely indifferent, and manifests no control over toilet habits. During this extreme he may experience the most vivid hallucinations particularly in regard to sin, punishment, and death.

As one can see, these symptoms indicate a profound disturbance calling for the best professional medical treatment. This is not to say that the patient might not recover without treatment. This frequently happens. But in such cases of spontaneous recovery, a recurrence of symptoms is almost a certainty.

Treatment can reduce the severity of the symptoms and assist the patient to return to normal. One of the most effective treatments for depression has been electroshock. "After a series of electroshock treatments the majority of depressed patients once again become animated and relatively normal and approachable." [1]

Chemotherapeutic drugs are also effective. Various tranquilizers may be used to reduce excitability during manic periods, and antidepressant drugs may be used for depressions. Psychotherapy is used effectively in conjunction with medical treatment.

The recovery rate for this disorder is very high.[2] Families can afford to be confident and optimistic when one of their members with a manic-depressive diagnosis is under skilled treatment.

Even so, they should be patient because recovery is usually slow, with the patient denying that he is improved, although all his behavior may indicate improvement.

Postpartum Depressions

It is difficult to place this classification correctly. These are depressive states of a mother following childbirth. Some of these states are mild and could more accurately be placed under the heading of a reactive or a neurotic depression. Sometimes the circumstances surrounding the birth, the condition of the mother, or the condition of the infant are in themselves stressful enough or disappointing enough to cause a mild depression which usually dissipates of itself or with the help of the attending physician. This can be complicated with endogenous factors to create a neurotic state which might call for extensive treatment.

But manic-depressive symptoms occur also. These would call for the types of treatment found to be helpful, as described above.

One type of preventive treatment suggested is that no

woman should have pregnancy and motherhood prescribed as an antidote to maladjustment.[3]

Another practical suggestion from the same source is that the mother, if depressed, be given sufficient help in caring for the infant, with emphasis upon the importance of the mother getting well.

Involutional Depressions

These states occur in women usually around the age of 50, in men around 60 or 65. The depression in women may take place prior to, during, or after the menopause. In men it seems to occur around the age of retirement.[4]

People with this disorder usually do not have the extreme swings of mood shown in the personality pattern of the manic-depressive. Rather the personality is rigid, extremely thrifty, stubborn, with few interests.

In women, the loss of youthful appearance and vigor, and the children growing up and leaving home may be factors in the emotional crisis.

In men, loss of accustomed activity on a job and feelings of futility accompanying this have something to do with the disturbance.

In either case, the situation may be complicated by declining vigor or poor health.

There are varying degrees of disturbances which may be associated with the involutional period. Some are relatively

mild and can be recovered from usually after simple sup-
portive therapy from a qualified physician. These, of course,
are not classified as mental illness.

The psychotic disturbance is manifested by any of a
number of severe symptoms, such as violent agitation, loss
of appetite, frequent digestive upsets, headaches, and great
difficulties in concentration.

The patient may have delusions of persecution and feel
that everyone, even those who love him most, are against
him. Hostility and self-condemnation are typical. The patient
feels overburdened and hopeless about his sins, and feels that
he is being punished for them.

Treatment for this psychosis may follow several lines already mentioned. Electroshock and chemotherapeutic measures have often been found to be effective.

In conclusion there is an optimistic note that can be
sounded. Treatment for various types of serious depressions
are becoming more and more effective. Progress is being
made in treating the whole person psychologically, socially,
and physically.

The reader will recognize that the discussion in this
chapter is an abbreviated one. Much has been left out. For
those who wish to read more widely on the subject, authori-
tative books are listed in the footnotes.

This brief treatment of the topic of severe depressions has
been written with the purpose of helping normally depressed
people to know that their depression is normal. It is also
hoped that those with serious symptoms will seek professional help at the earliest manifestations. The sooner treat-

ment begins for serious depressions, the better are the chances of recovery.

---

[1] Coleman, James C. *Abnormal Psychology and Modern Life.* Chicago: Scott, Foresman, & Co., p. 340.

[2] Bosselman, B.C. *Neurosis and Psychosis.* Springfield, Illinois: Charles Thomas, 1964, pp. 88-96.

[3] *Ibid.*, p. 143.

[4] *Ibid.*, pp. 144-149.

CHAPTER 22.

Arthur Cain's Global Attack on Personal Problems May Help You

WHAT WE ARE TRYING TO DO is to discover what can be done to better man's condition in all areas of his life. Improvement in one area usually spreads its benefits to other areas. What we would like to achieve is to bring man to his optimum performance in all areas.

What you are interested in is discovering how this constantly expanding knowledge affects you. What is there which you can apply to your own life that will make it happier, more harmonious, more productive, and more effective? You may rest assured that to the person who wishes to find these ways of self-improvement, the knowledge will be given. Perhaps acquiring the knowledge will come slowly over a period of years, but it is reassuring to know that the knowledge will certainly come to that person who seeks it.

One interesting and encouraging piece of work that is now being done is that of a clinical psychologist, Dr. Arthur H. Cain, who is extending a successful type of psychotherapy to alcoholics. And while you may never touch alcohol, the principles of his psychotherapeutic approach will give almost anybody an idea about the basic needs of human personality and how to fulfill them. Dr. Cain's therapy extends into practically every area of personality development.

Over a period of thirteen years, Dr. Cain has worked with thirty-nine alcoholics, many of whom were considered hopeless.[1] Most of them had tried other sources of help but were still alcoholics. Of the thirty-nine extreme cases, thirty-six recovered completely from alcoholism. This is a remarkable record.

Dr. Cain states that "these men and women are now sober, healthy, and successful in the new activities their new lives have made possible."

After reading about Dr. Cain's methods and his success, my personal opinion is that anyone, even the very well-adjusted, following a similar program, could improve himself measurably.

The program requires about twenty hours a week of each person's time. This, of course, is a great deal of time out of your week. If a person is working forty hours a week, and has a family to devote some of his time to, this would mean practically all his spare time.

The alcoholic is a seriously disturbed person. Perhaps for a less seriously disturbed person, less time might be required. For a well-balanced person who is striving for self-improvement on a long-range basis, the time required might depend upon how rapidly he wishes to improve. But it should be reemphasized here that self-improvement in any area will require time.

I am now in touch with several people who have launched themselves on programs of physical self-improvement. Most of these people have found that the minimum time in such a program if it is to yield good results is about an hour a day, five days a week. I know one entire family that spends this amount of time together walking and jogging. The family is together. They have a common goal. They enjoy each other's company as they work to reach the goal. But it does take time. Self-improvement is really fun, so most people are happy to spend the time required to gain such rich rewards.

This leads us logically into the first type of activity in which Dr. Cain's patients engage: physical training.[2] This part of the program encompasses health, personal appearance, and orderliness maintained in one's living and working places. Physical exercise programs are set up under the guidance of the alcoholic's (Dr. Cain calls them "colleagues") personal physician.

The colleague works at grooming and the improvement

of his personal appearance. He habitually keeps his surroundings both at home and at work neat and orderly.

The second type of activity is called educative counseling. This takes place once a week and requires two hours spent with a counselor. During the first hour, the colleague talks without interruption in a permissive atmosphere. Of the second hour, thirty minutes is spent with the counselor expressing his ideas about what the colleague had talked about and anything else relevant to the colleague's improvement. The final half hour is spent in a two-sided discussion of all that has gone before. During this part of the session both the colleague and the therapist feel freedom to communicate with each other about anything relating to the colleague's problems.

If you are considering adapting Dr. Cain's approach to your own development, this educative counseling could be worked out. An understanding friend might cooperate, or your pastor, or a church-school teacher. I have known a number of people who have found satisfactory people in their circle of acquaintances with whom free interaction was possible, fulfilling much of the function of Dr. Cain's educative counseling.

The next plank in Dr. Cain's therapeutic platform is reading. This is not merely reading for escape, nor for distraction, nor with the sole objective of pleasure. It is an intellectual activity planned to fill in gaps in the reader's knowledge, to "create new points of view, a new conception of himself and the world." The reading was largely philosophical in its content, including the religious.

Under the heading "organization" was the practice of keeping a diary. In the beginning, the colleague composed a master schedule for himself and the use of his time.

Perhaps you are seeing many parallels between Dr. Cain's approach to the problems of his alcoholics, and the system worked out by Success Motivation Institute discussed in Chapter 9. There are a great many parallels. You might be interested in returning to Chapter 9 to see just how close these parallels are.

Vocational guidance is a definite part of Dr. Cain's work. So many of his colleagues were misfits on their jobs. Naturally, if a person is in the wrong type of work, this can be the source of great trouble. To spend eight hours a day doing something unpleasant would make any worker an unhappy person.

Socialization is considered essential by Dr. Cain. This includes becoming a member of either some organized group or some informal group. The aim here is to generate "an interest in helping others." This is a distinctly Adlerian strategy found by Dr. Cain to have therapeutic value.

Aesthetics include a broad selection of activities—nature study, star-gazing—in short, anything related to the appreciation of, and meditation upon, beauty. Dr. Cain considers this important to well-rounded personality development.

The next area of personality development turned out to be one of the most important of all. This was called religious investigation. Dr. Cain evidently had the pragmatic view that usually a rational religious faith has a stabilizing effect upon the individual. Dr. Cain writes that he had been an "avowed agnostic." Apparently on a very practical basis he had his colleagues attend religious services of Protestant, Roman Catholic, and Jewish congregations.

This was part of "seeking truth." It was also to help the colleague determine if any of these groups and their beliefs and practices could assist the colleague in finding a "way of life." The quest was in the spirit of investigation to see if there was something in religion and if so, what, that might be found to benefit the colleague.

In the discussion resulting from the religious quest, Dr. Cain found himself at a disadvantage. Much of the vocabulary of religion was new to him. In order to be able to understand, Dr. Cain enrolled in a course in religion at Columbia University. In this course he found his learned instructor taking three apparent incompatibles, psychology, religion, and philosophy, and doing an adequate job of harmonizing them.

Dr. Cain and his colleagues at first approached the topics of religion only on an intellectual basis. But as they went deeper into the subject and realized that some of these concepts were just what they were looking for and needed, they faced the question, "What were we to do about them?"

In one paragraph the author writes that all the activities were important, but that reading was one of the more important because it, in turn, led to religious investigation and "it was through religious investigation that they (the colleagues) attained serenity."

The implication as we read between the lines is that Dr. Cain took his own medicine, too, and worked out for himself a positive religious philosophy. At least he became so convinced of the therapeutic benefits that later in his book he states that the disturbed person exemplified by his alcoholic colleague must be shown that there is more meaning to life than mere day-to-day existence. The disturbed person must be helped until he makes an about-face from egocentricity, hedonism, abnormal fears of pain and death, to a life that is "truth-centered," "other-directed," "dedicated," "God-centric."

A large number of people in the helping professions have discovered that a great deal of human apathy, low morale, depression, and a variety of their difficulties stem from the person not having found meaning in life. Quite evidently, a greater number of people find meaning through a satisfying religious philosophy than from any other source.

Dr. Cain's therapy is many faceted. It incorporates elements from other therapeutic methods, from religion, from philosophy, and many elemental common-sense features that build a person's self-respect and confidence.

One could predict that any person following a similar course of action, would discover himself improving in nearly every area of his life.

---

[1] Cain, Arthur H. *The Cured Alcoholic*. New York: The John Day Co., 1964, pp. 179-180.

[2] *Ibid.*, p. 185.

CHAPTER 23

You Can Find Your Own Strategies for Maintaining High Morale

MAINTAINING HIGH MORALE every day is a goal that is accessible to all of us. Each of us can work out his own practical strategy or combination of strategies by which he can sustain a habitual attitude of confidence which will help him live at his best.

In the preceding chapters we have used ideas from widely different sources, many of which are in fairly close agreement about what helps people.

Egocentricity versus Social Interest

Alfred Adler said that one major cause of much unhappiness and personality disturbance is egocentricity. To live a satisfying life, the "egocentric goal" must be broken up and one must begin to live a life of service in which he makes a contribution to others. All the religious approaches to self-improvement say the same thing: that loving others and showing this love by service gives lasting inner satisfactions. Success Motivation Institute suggests that to increase the efficiency and output of people working with you, you should "go out of your way to express your deep human feeling for each individual working for you."

Included in the therapy of Alcoholics Anonymous is working to help others overcome addiction to alcohol. And part of Arthur Cain's method of helping his colleagues is to get them interested in others and performing services for others.

Release from Excessive Tension

There is broad agreement among most of the authorities that "talking it out" or "writing it out" of your system is helpful. One can get a certain amount of release from harmful tension with these methods.

There are many ways of reducing excessive tensions. Almost any constructive method of self-expression such as music, painting, sculpture, and dancing bring positive results. Working at interesting hobbies usually achieves the same end. Physical exertion sustained for some time will also serve to reduce the harmful results of excessive emotional reactions. All of these activities are also distractors. They get your mind off your trouble and set up new chains of thought and feeling. There are many accessible activities that reduce tension, serve as distractors, and are in themselves rewarding.

Advantages of a Rational Religious Faith

The advantages of a rational religious faith are agreed upon by a surprising number of authorities engaged in the practical work of promoting mental and emotional health. This is one of the major emphases of Alcoholics Anonymous and became a large part of Arthur Cain's many-sided therapy with his disturbed colleagues. More and more churches are emphasizing the positive-thinking side of religion with great benefits to their members.

Personal Dividends from Relaxation

There is considerable scientific evidence for the benefits derived from learning Progressive Relaxation. Mental, emotional, and physical well-being all seem to result from the learned skill of being able at will to relax your entire body. Numerous therapists such as Drs. Haugen, Dixon, Wolpe, and Dickel use Progressive Relaxation as the basis for reconditioning patients to react with less anxiety to situations which previously produced a great deal of fearful tension.

Various Conditioning Procedures Have Good Results

There is also an accumulation of scientific support as a basis for conditioning procedures that help one establish a more constructive way of living. Verbal conditioning, which is one of the simplest, can build better morale in many situations.

All of the positive-thinking religions use verbal conditioning. Rational therapy employs it extensively. And in the business world Success Motivation Institute promotes verbal conditioning in many ways, from inspirational flashcards to which you expose yourself, to the tapes you listen to daily to give you a lift.

Autosuggestion is another method of verbal conditioning. Under conditions of relaxation and concentration, you give yourself positive verbal suggestions to be carried out in the future.

Many Agree on the Benefits of Self-analysis

Among a number of other authorities, Dr. Karen Horney advocated that self-analysis was practical, feasible, and safe.

However, she presented the psychoanalytic approach to self-analysis, which many people might feel is too deep for them. With this method one would record and try to interpret his dreams as well as his waking fantasies. He would also attempt to determine why he behaved as he did, particularly the undesirable ways of behaving.

Success Motivation Institute also includes self-analysis as a part of its morale-building courses. Here the method is direct and intensely practical. You develop self-understanding by writing down the answers to significant questions about yourself and every phase of your life and personality.

We see there are many connecting links between systems of self-help as set forward by psychologists, psychiatrists, certain religious groups, and an institute devoted largely to improving morale in business and industry.

There emerges here a clear and perhaps obvious principle. Your greatest self-improvement will doubtless result from improving yourself in every area of your life—the spiritual and ethical, the mental, emotional, esthetic, social, and physical. Improvement in one area facilitates improvement in all other areas.

You Can Develop Your Creative Potential

For the past decade there has been accelerated research among psychologists and educators in the field of creativity. Almost everybody apparently has creative potential. Walter J. Friess, of the A. C. Sparkplug Division of General Motors, has found that through the use of certain rather specific processes he can increase the creative output of their employees.

This comes as an encouraging word to adults. We might feel that children put in a favorable environment early would most likely develop creativity. But with adults, generally the attitude would be expressed in the trite proverb, "You can't teach an old dog new tricks." But W. J. Friess is demonstrating otherwise.

Developing your creative potential is definitely an antidote to the blues. When you are engaged in creative activity it is almost certain that you will be reducing depression. You will be busy in some type of work which you like to do for its own sake. The satisfactions deriving from this are strong antidepressants with nothing but good side-effects.

You Can Become a Self-actualizing Person

Very close akin to the emphasis put on creativity is a growing emphasis on self-actualization or self-fulfillment. People are born with all sorts of interesting potentialities.

Life can become a progressive development of these potentials. The person who has become the victim of habitual fear with the usual accompanying self-depreciation will live defensively. Energy that could be used constructively is wasted in the constant employment of defense mechanisms.

Perhaps all of us from time to time have employed numerous defenses. But in the process of maturing, it should become less and less necessary to live defensively.

One of the goals for mature personality development is that most of a person's energy should be directed toward self-enhancement rather than self-defensiveness.

The extreme of defensive living is the case of the person who grows more and more fearful until he cheats himself out of every interesting and useful activity. Cases of this kind are on record. One such person kept reducing activities until he finally confined himself behind the closed doors and windows of his own house, never even venturing into the yard. Fortunately, these extreme cases of defensiveness are rare. But there are multitudes of people with remarkably high potential who never develop it, but rather dissipate time and energy in ultradefensive living.

A common example of this is the person with "hurt feelings." Someone has made a remark in his presence that he feels was derogatory. The rest of the day is consumed with nursing his grievance over his hurt feelings and imagining all kinds of brilliant retorts he might have made. Here the person is uselessly throwing away time and energy on self-defensiveness.

As one grows better and better able to deal intelligently with his emotions, much of this waste can be eliminated. Energy and time can be employed efficiently and satisfyingly in working to reach definite goals that enrich life.

Practically all of the methods delineated in the chapters above are aimed at helping people achieve the goals they feel are right for them. Short-range goals are designed as rewarding in themselves, but even more valuable as steps toward the greater long-range goals.

We can become self-actualizing people. Our efforts during all our days can be aimed toward the goals we wish to achieve and can achieve.

The Last Word Is an Optimistic One

The last word, just like the first, is one of encouragement and confidence. What are some of the results you can achieve by finding and using the combination of methods of self-betterment which is right for you?

You can improve your health. Every function of your body can improve, including your nervous system, circulatory system, and your digestion. You can increase your vitality, stamina, and resistance against disease.

You can promote mental and emotional health. You can reduce worry and anxiety—perhaps eliminate them altogether. You can reduce harmful and excessive tensions and promote relaxed, contented living in which achievement comes not through damaging pressures but as the outcome of natural growth.

You can be revitalized and renewed from time to time, because our bodies, our minds, and our spirits are self-renewing if we give them the right climate for it.

You can be a person of faith and confidence rather than a fearful person. You can have a habitual confidence that will give you triumph instead of failure, and victory instead of defeat. You can have confidence that will assure you of success in the true meaning of the word, that of living a rich, satisfying life which contributes to your own well-being and that of your fellow men. Your life can be one of grace and goodness.

You can be a person loved and giving love. This is one of the basic goals of all living and it is one we deserve and can have. You can free yourself from bitterness, hostility and hard feeling. You can find warmth, affection, and friendship in great abundance.

You can have peace of mind that will spread to those around you. You can cultivate equanimity which from time to time will play a big part in the regenerative processes of your being, because it is from these deep wells of peace that life is renewed. You can become a complete stranger to needless fear and harmful fear. You can have the "peace that passes all understanding."

By discovering the truth about yourself and the truth about living, you can become, in a real sense, a free person. You can free yourself from everything that ever held you back or pulled you down. You can free yourself from failure and defeat. You can free yourself from a great deal of error. You can free yourself from ignorance and from worry and anxiety.

You can be the possessor of a transforming beauty. If life is lived right it is a beautiful process and the person living it is a beautiful person. You can walk in light and beauty, which is the heritage of the free spirit.

You can find abundant joy. Some of this may be wholesome elation, coming from the knowledge that life is good. You may know rapture in realizing your potential and in

finding your own people in the world. You may free yourself from gloom and the blues.

Your days can be days filled with courage, hope, and
high morale. Your experiences can become only those that
build faith and never weaken it.

This is your destiny and mine, to be people who walk in
dignity toward a goal that is always good because we make
it good. With this prospect before us, how can we do other
than succeed?

Index